THE TIMES

ENGLISH

STYLE

AND USAGE

GUIDE

THE  TIMES

ENGLISH

STYLE

AND USAGE

GUIDE

TIMES BOOKS

A Division of HarperCollins*Publishers*

First published by Times Books
A Division of HarperCollins*Publishers*
77–85 Fulham Palace Road
London W6 8JB

© Times Newspapers 1992

British Library Cataloguing-in-Publication Data
"Times" English Style and Usage Guide
I. Jenkins, Simon II. Ilson, Robert
428

ISBN 0-7230-0396-3

Typeset in Times Millennium by Times Newspapers

Printed in Great Britain

INTRODUCTION

English is not a language fixed for all time. Speech changes and its written form should change too. *The Times* must use the language of its readers, but that language at its best, clearest and most concise. The writing in a newspaper should also be consistent: hence the need for a style guide.

Most of the guidance is mandatory for staff writing in *The Times*, though some is permissive. Great writing may break rules but good writing does well to observe them. These rules are rooted in the essence of English grammar, in clarity and precision of meaning. Yet they also reflect changes in common English usage. They are meant to avoid pedantry.

The introductory remarks on aspects of style are expanded under the relevant heading in the alphabetical list. This is composed of words, phrases and common difficulties. The guidance applies to news, comment and feature pages. There are bound to be exceptions, for instance for arts and diary pages and for letters to the editor and outside contributors. But remember, inconsistency in style is unsettling and irritates readers. Where the guide conflicts with *The Oxford Dictionary for Writers and Editors* the guide should take precedence, but the *Dictionary* should be consulted where the guide is silent.

Brevity A writer's most precious commodity is space. Space is time for writer and reader alike. Verbosity clouds meaning. Brevity is always a virtue, in phrases, sentences, whole passages of writing. So use short rather than long words. Words with an Anglo-Saxon root are usually clearer and shorter than Latin-Norman ones: "be" rather than "exist", "go" rather than "proceed", "know" rather than "comprehend". Modern writing is cursed with overblown words and phrases. Whenever you write a long word, ponder a short one instead.

Verbs The verb is the engine of a sentence. Keep it working flat out. A good verb is the writer's best friend; use a dull one and the sentence will stumble. Always try to use active rather than passive verbs, transitive rather than intransitive verbs. Remember that modifying adverbs can weaken as well as strengthen verbs, hence *Catch-22*: "Death to all qualifiers!". Like adjectives, adverbs are an indulgence, often a sign that noun and verb are not working properly. A well-chosen verb should be able to dispense with modifiers: try changing a verb before conceding a modifier. "The bus accelerated swiftly down the hill and was involved in a collision with a lorry" should be "The bus sped downhill and hit a lorry".

Abstraction Try to avoid abstract nouns. Newspapers are about what people and things do and have done to them. They should use concrete words. Abstract nouns and phrases are often an escape from precise meaning. They are easier to use and thus a sign of lazy writing. A headline is usually killed by an abstract noun. Hence the guide's aversion to words such as situation, crisis, problem, resolution, question, condition.

Punctuation No newspaper sentence should be confusing or open to double meaning. No paragraph should need to be read twice. Every sentence other than an exclamation should have a subject and a verb. The best punctuation is the full stop. Commas should usually be kept for punctuating lists and breaking up sentences to avoid confusion. They should not join sentences that are better separated by a full stop. Semi-colons usually look messy and are best confined to separating lists of phrases. Colons have a specific use, throwing meaning forward. Dashes are a bad habit, often used to pursue a line of thought that the writer cannot be bothered to construct some other way. Dashes also look ugly in a column of type. Brevity is all.

Conjunctions Avoid unnecessary buts, ands, howevers, yets. A well-steered sentence should convey its own contrasts of meaning with verbs and nouns. It should not need the tugboat of a conjunction. Always revise a sentence to see what conjunctions can be removed.

Paragraphing A paragraph, says Gowers, is "a unit of thought, not of length ... homogeneous in subject matter and sequential in treatment of it". Rarely should a paragraph in *The Times* be of only one sentence, least of all a short one, unless special emphasis is needed. Long paragraphs are tedious but short ones are jerky and can be equally hard to follow. The best advice is to remember Gowers and ask, before pressing the paragraph key, "Have I finished that thought?"

Quotations The sloppy use of quotes is the bane of good writing. A well-chosen quote can electrify a passage. Equally it can distort what a speaker said. As a rule, a quote must be attributed to a person, with full name and the date and place of quotation. Unattributed quotes are normally banned. Where they proliferate, for instance in the more pedestrian political reporting, they should be treated with caution. Many readers are inclined to believe they are made up. *The Times* should conform to the code of practice now common in America. An unattributed quote should be used only where confidentiality is clearly essential, not merely to add spice or colour to a story. Even then, the writer should know the source and be prepared to inform the editor of it. Except in extreme cases, unattributed quotes should never be derogatory of individuals or named institutions. Such quotes are cowardly and read as such. If common gossip of a critical nature needs to be reported and a source is not willing to be quoted on the record, some indirect way of conveying the information must be used so that the writer bears the burden of judging that the material merits dissemination. Never

make up a quote from fragments of quotes or cuttings.
Such a practice is unethical and legally dangerous.

Headlines Headlines are journalism at its most
refined. They must encapsulate both the message of an
article and its stamp of quality. They are acutely
vulnerable to mistakes, solecisms and clichés and
require greater attention than any text. The old rules
are the best: always use a noun and an active verb;
avoid adjectives and modifiers; use concrete not abstract
nouns; express one message, not two linked by a tired
conjunction like "as" (unless the link is dramatic: "Nero
fiddles as Rome burns"). Omit titles and try to avoid
definite and indefinite articles, numbers and initials.
Above all, avoid headline clichés: "get under way", "set
to", "looms", and hyperboles such as crisis, crash, snub,
hit, slam.

Style Read the masters on style, especially Fowler and
Gowers. Style is the essence of clear writing. A journalist
ignorant of style, of words and their usage, is untrained
and illiterate. Good style is hard work. A conscientious
writer should revise every article until each word is
fashioned to the job with clarity and economy. Only
then should it be offered to the reader.

Reference books The following are essential tools, as is a good general encyclopaedia.

Collins English Dictionary (HarperCollins)

The Complete Plain Words Sir Ernest Gowers (HMSO, Penguin)

A Dictionary of Modern English Usage H.W. Fowler, 2nd edn revised by Sir Ernest Gowers (Oxford University Press)

The Oxford Dictionary for Writers and Editors (Oxford University Press)

The Times Atlas of the World, Comprehensive Edition (Times Books)

Webster's New Geographical Dictionary (Merriam-Webster)

Who's Who (A & C Black)

A

a, an the fundamental rule is to use *a* before consonants and *an* before vowels. But *a* is to be used, not *an*, before all words beginning with a vowel or diphthong having the sound of the *u* in unit, and generally before an aspirated *h* (with certain exceptions). Thus *a* eulogy, European, hero, history, hope, hospital, unanimous, university, useful. Always use *an* before unaspirated *h*; thus *an* heir, honest, honour, hour. Sometimes *an* is also used before the aspirated *h* when the syllable containing the *h* is unaccented; thus *an* heroic (yet *a* hero), *an* hotel, *an* historical event (but *a* history book). Nowadays this is an affectation, permissible but not *Times* style.

abbreviations and contractions see **appellations**, **initials** and under relevant subject, eg **military**, **naval**, **scientific measurements**, etc.

Abdul be careful, this means "slave of ..." and must therefore be used between a first name and surname. Similarly, *abu* means "father of ..." and requires a surname. Break such words at *Abd-*, not at *Ab-*. See also **Arab names**.

accents care must be taken to give French, German, Italian, Spanish and Ancient Greek words their proper accents and diacritical marks. Omit accents in other languages unless you are sure of them. There are no accents in Latin. Beware: the French regularly change their accent rules, and are debating the future of the circumflex. Since there are no accents in English, French words that have taken English nationality should drop their accents (hotel, depot, menage, regime). If, however, the accent makes a crucial difference to pronunciation (final *é* in particular) it should be retained (communiqué, habitué, fiancée).

Where one accent is for this reason retained the word must be given all the accents due to it in French (mêlée, émigré, protégé). The accent should be kept on *à* (as in vis-à-vis) to distinguish the French preposition from the English indefinite article. The cedilla should also be kept, as in façade. Accents and diacritical marks need not be used in headlines. See also **foreign words**, **italics**.

accommodation a long, dull word best avoided. Accommodate is even worse. Write what you mean: seats, rooms, or help, contain.

acknowledgment no *e* before *-ment*.

actors refers generically. You need not say actors and actresses.

acts (parliamentary), these have capital letters when their correct titles are being used, but generic acts and all bills do not; thus, the proposed abortion bill, the safety acts, but the Finance Act.

AD, BC AD comes before the date: AD 350. BC comes after: 350 BC. Both are used after the word century, as in "first century BC".

addresses Pennington Street, unabbreviated. Numbers are generally omitted; when they must be given, use no comma: 1 Virginia Street.

adjectives beware of adjectives that spring automatically to mind as soon as their noun is mentioned: serious danger, widespread concern, acute crisis, considerable difficulty, active consideration, essential condition, substantial majority, long-felt want, all-time record. If the noun looks naked without its protective adjective, let it go naked. It may even be more arresting that way. "Cultivate the habit of reserving adjectives to make your meaning more precise, and suspect those you find yourself using to make it more emphatic" (Gowers). Emphasis and descriptive force should come from the correct verb and noun. See also **Introduction**, **clichés**, **imagery**.

adverbs before using an adverb to strengthen a verb, try changing to another verb to achieve the same effect: "he went quickly" to "he hurried". Rarely start a sentence (except this one), let alone a paragraph, with an adverb: "Interestingly ...", "Ironically ...", etc. Such constructions are not forbidden, but sentences starting with adverbs are normally built on sand.

Afrikaans is a language, the people are Afrikaners.

aged, aging, old the polite word is elderly, though this too is sensitive. Avoid for people under 65.

ages are given between commas: John Smith, 32, a journalist (no parentheses).

Aids not a disease but a medical condition. Diseases that affect people who are HIV positive may be called "Aids-related diseases". Avoid "died of Aids".

air force use lc except in full name: US Air Force, Royal Air Force. Abbreviations: Air Vice-Marshal, AVM; Air Commodore, Air Cdre; Group Captain, Gp Capt; Wing Commander, Wg Cdr; Squadron Leader, Sqn Ldr; Flight Lieutenant, Flt Lt; Flying Officer, FO; Pilot Officer, PO; Flight Sergeant, FS; Chief Technician, Chief Tech; Sergeant, Sgt; Corporal, Cpl; Junior Technician, Jnr Tech; Senior Aircraftman/woman, SAC/SACW; Leading Aircraftman/woman, LAC/LACW. The Master Air Crew: Master Air Electronics Officer, MAEO; Master

Air Loadmaster, MALM; Master Signaller, M Sig. See also **military nomenclature**.

Alastair always check the spelling of this wayward name.

A level, O level separate out as noun, hyphenate when adjective, no inverted commas.

alibi is not a general alternative to *excuse*. It means being elsewhere at the material time.

allege alarm bells should ring when you think of using it. Avoid any suggestion that the writer is making the allegation. Specify the source of an allegation. Use "alleged bribe" or a similar phrase when necessary to make it clear that an unproved action is not being treated as fact. Be sure that the source of the charge is specified elsewhere in the story. Avoid redundant uses, eg: "The prosecution accused her of allegedly posing as a rural dean". Do not use alleged as a hack qualifier. Instead, use something like apparent, ostensible or reputed. Do not use alleged before an event that is known to have occurred, when the dispute is over who participated in it. Do not write: "He attended the alleged meeting", when what you mean is: "He allegedly attended the meeting".

all right never alright.

all-time avoid the compound adjective "all-time" and especially "all-time high". Say highest.

All Souls College Oxford no apostrophe.

alsatian (dog) is spelt thus. The correct name of the breed is German Shepherd.

American a source of much confusion and debate. The word refers to two continents. Canadians, Mexicans, etc are upset when it is used to refer only to the United States of America. Yet common usage does just this. The initials US also look clumsy, except in headlines. In general, use American where spoken English would do so: American spokesman, company, actor, food. But use US where there is the slightest risk of confusion with Canadian or Latin American, and also with government institutions: US Congress, US Secretary of State, US Navy, US military operation. American president is permitted.

Americanisms do not use as alternatives to an English phrase, as in "get to go" or "set to move". Some are now standard usage, such as ballpark, smug, brunch.

American spellings the titles of American institutions, etc that contain words of which the American spelling is different from the English (eg, Secretary of Defense, American Federation of Labor) should be written in *The Times* with English spellings: Secretary of Defence, American Federation of Labour.

amid not amidst.

among not amongst.

ampersands should be used only in the title of a company, as Marks & Spencer. Do not space the symbol between initials: P&O.

amok not amock or amuck.

and see **punctuation**.

and also never use together.

Anglo- prefix meaning English. While it is common usage for Britain as a whole — eg, in Anglo-French relations — it can offend non-English Britons. Use carefully. See also **Britain, England**.

annual an event cannot be described as annual until it has been held in at least two successive years. Do not use the phrase "first annual". Instead, say that somebody plans to hold an event annually.

anticipate not to be used for *expect*. To anticipate a large audience means (or should mean) to get in in front of it, not to expect it. But it can mean to "expect and take appropriate action about". To anticipate marriage is different from expecting to marry.

anti-Semitic, anti-Semitism to be spelt thus.

apostrophe this causes much trouble. Its use as a genitive is relatively simple, singular *'s*, plural *s'*. With words ending in *s* that are singular, follow the rule of writing what is voiced: Keats's poetry, *The Times*'s style (or *Times* style), but Achilles' heel. (Fowler's famous horror — in '*The Times*'s' opinion — is a good example of why too much punctuation is ugly.) An apostrophe indicates the plural of single letters — p's and q's — but should be avoided as a plural of groups of letters/numbers. Thus MPs, 1960s to 1990s. Avoid using an apostrophe to abbreviate *do not* and *it is*. *Don't, it's, shan't* are messy colloquialisms that should be confined to quotes.

appellations almost every surname should be granted the courtesy of a title. The exceptions are convicted offenders, the dead (but not the recently dead), and cases where common usage omits a title: most on the arts, sport, books and diary pages. Here men and women should be treated equally: if Olivier, then

Dench. On news pages, sportsmen, artists, authors, etc should normally be given a title, even if it sometimes looks odd. Otherwise, proceed as follows. On first mention, the titles Mr, Mrs and Miss should be omitted: use first name and surname alone, changing to Mr Jones, Miss Jones on subsequent mentions. Avoid initials and middle initials unless the person is best-known thereby, eg, W.G. Grace (with full points).

Unmarried women are Miss, as are women who wish to be known by their maiden names. Only where they wish to be known as Ms or some other appellation should this rule be set aside. In stories originating in America, however, use Ms in preference to Miss unless requested otherwise.

Married couples Beware the use of possessives in stories about married couples. Avoid the phrase "Mr John Jones and his wife". Say Mr and Mrs John Jones, or preferably John and Mary Jones, or Mary and John Jones where the wife is more relevant to the story.

Doctor A person wishing to be called Dr, with a doctorate from a reputable university, can be referred to as such even if not a medical doctor.

Young people Persons up to the age of 18 are not normally accorded Mr, Mrs or Miss, but if a girl is married she should be called Mrs. Males in this group should normally be called boys (unless, for instance, they are soldiers); if 18 or over, men. The distinction is less rigid in the case of girls and women, but avoid calling all females girls, particularly unmarried ones who are not yet middle-aged. The term youth for an individual should be discouraged, and teenager should be used with discretion.

Court proceedings Accused persons should be accorded the appropriate title, after the name has been given fully in the charge or summons. Only convicted persons should be referred to by surname alone.

Foreign appellations The subject of foreign appellations is often reviewed. We keep some to convey

the international flavour of foreign news. Use local
honorifics in the main European countries and Latin
America. To try for more would be complicated and
reach the point where their inclusion would be
confusing. The question has been asked why French
titles are not accorded to Francophone Africa when
Latin American stories use Spanish and Portuguese
ones. The answer is that Spanish and Portuguese have
become the common language of all but a small
minority in Latin America but French is more the
language of the elite in the former African colonies. The
same applies to Angola, Mozambique, etc.

France: M, Mme, Mlle and Me for Maître (legal)
Germany and Austria: Herr, Frau, Fräulein
Spain and all Spanish-speaking Latin American
countries: Señor, Señora, Señorita
Italy: Signor, Signora, Signorina
Portugal and Brazil: Senhor, Senhora (but not
Senhorinha)

This applies to the people of those countries, even when
they are resident elsewhere, unless they have clearly
adopted the nationality of another country. The use of
Fräulein, Señorita and Signorina for Miss is not as
strict as in this country and should be confined to young
unmarried women and actresses.

For all other nationalities, use English style except
where it is possible to use a local title (Ayatollah,
Begum, Chief, Pandit, Pir, Sardar, Shaikh, etc, but *not*
Sayed) or a military one, as in Colonel Gaddafi. Some
titles and honorifics may be of such general usage as to
break these rules, and where anyone specifically
requests a certain style that should be respected, eg,
Baron in Germany.

Beware the following:

Burma: U means Mr and Daw means Mrs.

China: use the first Chinese name as the surname.
Deng Xiaoping becomes Mr Deng.

Malaysia: Encik means Mr, Puan means Mrs and Cik means Miss.

See also **Arab names**, **courts**, **military nomenclature**, **naval nomenclature**, **peers**, **titles**.

appendix plural appendices, but appendixes in anatomy.

apropos of avoid.

Arab to be used always with care. Seek advice from an expert according to context.

Arab names there is no agreed system of transliterating Arabic that will both give an idea of how names should be pronounced and satisfy the experts. All we seek is consistency. The following notes refer also to Urdu (Bangladesh, parts of India, Pakistan), which uses the same lettering system.

1 The familiar and simple are to be preferred to the strange: caliph, Koran, Mecca. Many names with a familiar appearance, particularly from Syria/Lebanon and the Maghreb, retain gallicisms misleading in an English context. Some are so firmly established, or are the form adopted by the holders (eg, Bourguiba, Chamoun, Suez), that they cannot be changed. But gallicisms such as *ou* (prefer *u*), *ch* (*sh*) and *eh* (terminal *a*) should be avoided where possible, thus Hijaz not Hedjaz, Yusif not Youssef, for example.

2 Consonants. Arabic contains all English consonants except *p*, *v* and *x*. It also contains some extra ones. These can be ignored apart from:

   gh, distinct from *g* alone, eg, Baghdad, Maghreb, but Amin Gemayel. Remember that hard *g* standing alone is (almost invariably) the Egyptian for what is elsewhere pronounced as soft *j*, eg, gallabiya and jellaba, Egyptian/non-Egyptian versions of the smock-like dress; gebel/jebel for hill. Prefer *j* outside Egypt.

kh, distinct from *k* alone, eg, *Allahu akbar* (God is great), but *Akhbar al-Yom* (*Daily News*).

q, distinct guttural form of *k* and established in words like Iraq, Aqaba.

To be retained:

h, pronounced distinctly in Arabic even where English might expect a linked sound, as in the guerrilla movement Fath (best spelling, but Fatah is accepted usage). Fahd is similar, and needs no vowel before the *d*.

d, *dh*, *z*, which are different letters in Arabic, but there is confusion about transliteration since the sounds vary regionally. Aim for simplicity, preferring *d* or *z*: Fadil not Fadhl, Nadim not Nadhim.

glottal stop, common in Arabic but virtually unpronounceable in English. Delete apostrophe transliteration: Baath not Ba'ath, Jaafar not Ja'afar, Said not Sa'id.

doubled consonants, as important for Arabic pronunciation as for Italian, but it is hopeless to expect to find them always present. Muhammad is correct *Times* style for the Prophet, but respect the many other spellings of this name (Mahmud is a different name). Nasser and Kassim achieved a double *s* to which they were not entitled, giving the impression that the preceding vowel is short, whereas it should be long. Nasir and Qasim are correct, and should be used for future holders of these names. See also **Gaddafi**.

3 Vowels. There are only three vowels in written Arabic, *a*, *i* and *u*, each with long and short forms. Strictly speaking, *e* and *o* have no place, but it is impossible to keep them out: eg, Bedu, Emir, Oman, Omdurman, Osman, Yemen, etc. Always prefer *a* and *i* to *e*, and *u* to *o*, and avoid the gallic *ou*, since *u* is sufficient: Khartum, Mahmud, Sudan. Similarly, use *i* not *ee* for the long *i* (fellahin, not fellaheen), and prefer *i* to *y* at the end of a word: Fahmi, Sabri, Shukri, not

Sabry, etc.

diphthongs There are two, *ai* and *au* (or *aw*). Following the logic above, use *ai* rather than *ei*: Bahrain, Husain, Kuwait, Shaikh (but use Saddam Hussein, ie, the gallic version). Similarly, Fawzi not Fowzi, Taufiq not Tewfiq or Towfig.

endings Many words have a weak ending confusingly found transliterated *ah, eh, er, ir, a, e, i*. Common usage apart, *a* is best, eg, Nayariya rather than Nahariyeh.

4 Names with *al-*, *Abdul*. Many family names contain *al-* or *Abdul*. These may cause confusion.

  a The *l* in *al-* ("the") elides before some consonants (*s, d, r, n, t, z*, etc), so Nuri al-Said and Samir al-Rifai are pronounced Nuri Assaid and Samir Arrifai and are often so written. Others, usually ending in Din (religion) may go further and combine all three parts of the name into one (eg, Nur al-Din becomes Nuraddin and Azhar al-Din, cricketer, Azharuddin). In both cases the first form is to be preferred, however, the *al-* being lc and hyphenated to the following capital letter.

  b *Abdul* (properly *abd al-* ... "slave of ...") can never stand alone but demands another name as slave-master, eg, Aziz, Majid, Rahman, etc; the whole then forms an indivisible surname, eg, Samir Abd al-Rahman, Walid Abd al-Aziz, etc. After first mention these should become Mr Abd al-Rahman, Mr Abd al-Aziz rather than the variant Abdurrahman, etc. Note that Abdullah and Abdulilah are distinct names.

  c The converse of **b** is to be watched: names like Rahman and Aziz usually demand an *Abd al-* before them. It is technically as incorrect to refer to Nasser (rather than Abd al-Nasser) as it would be to speak of Paul Sartre instead of Jean-Paul Sartre, or, more exactly, to refer to Tholemew and Dore instead of Bartholemew and Theodore. Inevitably, in such established cases as President Nasser, simplicity wins over accuracy.

5 Iraqi names. In Iraq more than in most Arab countries, names of Turkish origin survive, eg, Chadirchi, Pachachi. Here it is permissible to use the letters *ch, e, p*, which would be incorrect in true Arabic.

Arafat, Yassir not Yasser.

arbitrate, mediate terms in industrial negotiations that have different meanings. Do not confuse them. An arbitrator hears evidence from all persons concerned, then hands down a decision. Somebody who mediates listens to arguments of all parties, and tries by the exercise of reason or arm-twisting to bring them to an agreement.

archaeologist not *arche-*.

Argentine as adjective, but Argentinian as person. The country is Argentina, not the Argentine.

argue awful synonym of *said*, especially in features by-lines.

army but British Army. For ranks, etc, see also **military nomenclature**.

artifact not artefact.

artiste an entertainer of either sex. It is preferable to say singer, dancer, conjurer, actor, etc,.

as at April 1 say "on April 1", unless you wish to imply something is about to change.

ascendancy lc, but when referring to a specific period of Irish history, the Ascendancy.

as follows never as follow.

assassin see **killer**.

assure you *assure* your life; *ensure* means to make certain; you *insure* against risk.

at the present time why not *now*? Avoid the phrase "as of now".

at this time use *now*.

attorney-general plural attorneys-general.

Auditor General no hyphen.

Auto-immune deficiency see **Aids**.

ay (yes), aye (ever), Ayes (debate).

B

back benches (parliamentary), two words, but backbenchers, backbench revolt.

bail from prison, but bale out of an aircraft.

balk not baulk.

bank holiday takes lc.

bar use uc for legal profession (the Bar), and for the Bar *of* the House of Commons, but there are other bars *in* the Houses of Parliament.

basis "on a ... basis" is overworked. In most cases a simple adverbial or prepositional phrase is better. For "he accepted employment on a part-time basis" say "he accepted part-time employment".

BC goes after the figure, AD before. See **AD**.

Beaufort scale wind speeds from 0 to 12 (use numerals), but Americans use the scale to 17. See also **wind**.

Becket, St Thomas not à Becket.

Beduin is plural. The singular is Bedu.

beg the question do not confuse with "ask the question".

benefited like balloted and budgeted, has only one *t*.

-berg, -burg always check spelling of towns with these endings, and those ending in *-borough*, *-brough*.

Bermudian a person from Bermuda (not Bermudan).

best man "Mr Jones was best man", not "the best man was Mr Jones".

between use "between 20,000 and 25,000" or "from 20,000 to 25,000", not "between ... to ...".

bi- beware of attaching this prefix to English words of time. It is ambiguous. Bi-monthly might mean twice monthly or every two months. *Bi-* is correctly used in Latin compounds (bicentenary, biennial, etc) where it has the force of two, not half. Biannual means twice a year, but should be avoided as confusing. Write "twice a year" or "every two years".

biased has only one *s*.

Bible takes uc but biblical is lc.

biblical references thus: II Corinthians ii, 2;
Luke iv, 5.

bid a financial offer, whether for a pot at Sotheby's or a
company on the Stock Exchange. It does not mean
attempt, except in headlines.

bill (parliamentary), always lc until it becomes an act,
for which see **acts**.

billion nowadays equals a thousand million, not a
million million; style is 1 billion, £15 billion (bn in
headlines). See also **numbers**.

biological terms frequent mistakes occur in *The Times*
in the printing of scientific names of animals and
plants, especially in the use of capital or lower-case
initial letters. The scientific name of every animal or
plant consists of two words. The first indicates the
genus, the second the species within that genus. This
system, which has existed since the time of Linnaeus, is
called the binomial system. In zoology a trinomial
system, with an added third word to denote a difference
less than specific, is in use. It is seldom necessary to
employ the trinomial system in a newspaper.

All scientific names are printed in italics and the
first word, or generic name, is always written with a
capital. The second word is always written with a lower-
case initial, eg, *Erythronium dens-canis* (common
name: Dog's-tooth Violet, uc). Most modern botanists
follow this practice, but follow copy in signed
contributions from botanists of standing. When generic
names are used by themselves, be guided by common
sense: rhododendron has become anglicised in use and
and should be used with a lower-case initial and not in
italics. When, however, some scientific flavour still
adheres to the word, as in a sentence such as "He
announced the discovery of several new species of

Thalictrum", the more formal style of capital and italics should be retained.

birthday people and other animals have birthdays, everything else has anniversaries.

bisexual pronouns *he, his* can no longer refer to both sexes equally. This causes writers great difficulty. The form "he or she" will sometimes do, as on occasions (see entry for doctors) will the substitute of the plural *they*: "Everybody should bring their lunch ...". Or reconstruct the sentence avoiding the obstacle.

blacks (people), lc, strictly refers to Negroes. Remember that many Asians and people of mixed race ("coloureds") do not wish to be called black. Black is being replaced by Afro-Caribbean or, in America, by African-American. *The Times* should follow customary usage in this sensitive area. The word coloured is falling into disuse. In South Africa it denotes mixed race and should take a capital C, omitting the phrase "mixed race" after it. References to race should be used only where relevant to the sense of the story. See also **Coloureds**.

block not bloc (eg, power block).

blue an "Oxbridge" sportsman, lc.

boat a boat is a water craft of any size. A ship is a large, sea-going vessel, big enough to carry smaller boats. In the Royal Navy, submarines are called boats.

bogey (golf), bogie (wheels), bogy (ghost).

Bolshevik is spelt thus.

borstals no longer exist. They are now called Young

25

Offender Institutions.

both use only where necessary, not as in "they both met". *Both* must be followed by *and* and each word must embrace common parts: "both in Britain and in France". Never follow *both* with "as well as".

boy friend two words. Avoid using the word lover unless a measure of secrecy and subterfuge is implied. Use boy friend only for young people, otherwise man friend or just friend where the gender is obvious. The word partner is increasingly used to describe a long-term relationship between two people who have not married.

Boy Scouts are now simply Scouts in the UK. See **Scouts**.

brackets strictly speaking, the term brackets means square brackets only, but is nowadays interchangeable with parentheses. Brackets usually enclose a passage within quotes to indicate words not quoted but needed to assist the meaning. See also **parentheses**.

Brit, Britisher not to be used; Briton, if necessary.

Britain or Great Britain = England, Wales and Scotland. United Kingdom = Britain and Northern Ireland. British Isles = United Kingdom and the Republic of Ireland, Isle of Man and Channel Islands. These distinctions are most important. Sloppy use of England for Britain and vice versa offends non-English Britons. Stories about England (and Wales) may not apply to Scotland and Northern Ireland; for instance, national statistics, local government, Whitehall regulations. Always check this before writing a story.

broadcast not broadcasted.

broadcasting includes both sound and television, either of which can be specified. Do not contrast broadcasting with television.

broadsheet this neutral word is preferable to *quality* in describing serious British newspapers. See also **quality press**, **tabloid**.

budget lc, except in reference to the Chancellor of the Exchequer's official Budget; budgeted (verb) has one *t*.

bullion is gold or silver in unminted form.

burgomaster or chief burgomaster of a German city, not mayor.

Burma not Myanmar.

Burmese are inhabitants of Burma, Burmans are a Burmese people.

burnt not burned.

Bushey, Hertfordshire; Bushy Park, near Hampton Court.

by, by- bylaw, bypass, byroad but by-election, by-product.

C

cabinet, the lc, but Cabinet Office takes uc.

Caernarvon but Lord Carnarvon.

cagey, cagily American for wary, warily; avoid except in direct quotation.

call-up (noun), call up (verb).

Cambridge see **Oxford and Cambridge**.

canvas (material); canvass (votes, etc) is both noun and verb.

Cape Town two words, both uc.

capitalisation this is the source of great tribulation. Please adhere to the following guidance. Too many capital letters are ugly. Capitals interrupt the passage of the eye along a line. They are often unnecessary, especially with non-proper nouns such as government or ministry. Struggle to avoid them unless to do so looks absurd. If in doubt use lower case. In general, the proper names of people, their formal titles and the names of well-known and substantial institutions require capitals.

Job titles and descriptions Most job titles are lower case where the name of the job is essentially descriptive (prime minister, foreign secretary), but upper case where it reflects an honorific title (Lord Chancellor) or could be confusing (Mr Speaker). The names of lesser organisations are lower case, as are generic institutions such as committees or councils. This approach makes more sense than all other, superficially sensible, approaches. Individual cases are discussed under their own entries but here are some examples of the guidance in practice.

President is a title but also a job description: thus President Bush, but George Bush, the president. Prime minister is not a title in Britain. Never write Prime Minister Major but always Mr Major, the prime minister. The following jobs and names take uc: Lord Chancellor, Archbishop of Canterbury, Chancellor of

the Exchequer, Secretary of State, Chief Whip (but an
assistant whip, lc), Department of Education, Ministry
of Defence, Foreign Office, House of Commons,
Parliament (when referring to Britain's but not to
foreign ones: a rare chauvinist distinction), Norwich
City Council, Labour's National Executive Committee.
The following are lc: minister, leader, ministry, foreign
secretary, defence secretary, general and admiral (when
not used as titles), Arsenal football club (except where
the club is a plc), the city council (in Norwich).

Government and institutions The words
government, administration and cabinet are always lc,
unless part of an official title, such as Government
House or Her Majesty's Government or the Cabinet
Office. Government in Britain is constitutionally a
seamless web, from ministers of the Crown, through
cabinets and departments to lowly clerks. There is no
confusion here and no distinction should be drawn
between different tiers by capitalisation. The only mild
oddity is when government is used near Opposition,
which requires a capital to avoid confusion. You must
endure this oddity: "The leader of the Opposition
replied to the government minister"

The word party is lc except where the party's title is
incomplete without the word and/or the party is
customarily known by initials including Party: thus
Labour party, Conservative party but Social and
Democratic Labour Party (SDLP).

When spelling out capitalised abbreviations such as
CAP (common agricultural policy) use lc.

To avoid too many capitals, try to turn institutions
from proper to common nouns: education department
rather than Department of Education, defence secretary
rather than Secretary of State for Defence.

Royal family Her Majesty the Queen (usually just
"the Queen") is uc, as is the Sovereign (to avoid
confusion). But Prince Charles becomes "the prince".
See also **titles**.

29

Compass points Places are obviously capitalised, but north, south, west and east are not, except in place-names and where political in character or referring to well-known regions. Thus the American South, East-West relations, East Anglia, the North West, South Wales, but eastern Britain or firms moving north. East(ern) and West(ern) Europe are still sufficiently distinct regional entitles to merit capitalised status, though this may change. See also **place-names**.

Derivatives Capitalise words that are derived from a proper noun and still depend on it for their meaning: Christian, English, French, Freudian, Marxism, Shakespearean. Words derived from a proper noun but no longer dependent on it for their meanings eventually lose their capitals: malapropism, quixotic, venetian blind. The word communist causes trouble: it normally takes lc except in reference to the party or when used adjectivally in this institutional sense. See also under specific words.

carry out the word *do* is often better: "The work was done".

case a much overworked word. "In many cases" may be "in many places" or just "often". "In the case of" can nearly always be avoided. "Is it the case that?" means "Can ...?".

category is best kept for logic. Use class, kind, sort, type.

cater for the primary meaning is to supply food for. It has legitimate metaphorical extensions, but they should be used sparingly.

Catherine always check the spelling. The Catherine wheel is named after St Catherine of Alexandria.

Catholic it is necessary to say Roman Catholic on first mention, then Catholic alone. The adjective catholic (lc) has a different meaning. See also **church**.

ceilidh social gathering (Highland).

cello short for violoncello, has no apostrophe.

celsius, centigrade use either. Use both celsius and fahrenheit in news stories. See also **degrees**, **temperature**.

centenaries centenary, bicentenary, tercentenary. After that say four (five, etc) hundredth anniversary.

centring but centering of arches in bridge building.

Ceylon now Sri Lanka, Sri Lankan. The Sinhalese are the majority group.

chairman still common usage referring to men and women, except in quotes. Do not use "the chair" or "chairperson" except in quotes, or in the phrase "address your remarks to the chair".

Chancellor of the Exchequer is uc. See also **capitalisation**.

changeover is usually an unnecessary variant of *change*.

Channel tunnel (one uc, one lc); do not use Chunnel.

chaos a strong word, grossly overworked. The word disorder or confusion is usually adequate. Chaos should be avoided in *The Times*, at least until the arrival of Armageddon, when it will be permissible.

charge that American for allege that. Avoid except in proper legal sense: "You are charged that, on Saturday...".

cheap goods are cheap, prices are low.

Chekhov to be spelt thus.

chess king, queen, etc are lc. Beware chess metaphors. A match is a series, not a game. Never "castle out of check", which is not allowed in chess. Talks cannot reach stalemate and "continue tomorrow". Pawns are so abused by journalists as to be beyond stylistic protection.

Chinese names use the English (Wade-Giles, not Pinyin) style for Canton, China, Chou En-lai, Mao Tse-tung, Mongolia, Nanking, Peking, Shanghai and Tibet. See also **place-names**.

chip now common usage for microchip.

Christ Church Oxford two words, do not add College.

Christchurch one word, towns in Hampshire and in New Zealand.

christened people are christened, boats and ships and trains are named.

Christian, Christianity unchristian, non-Christian, antichristian, Antichrist, ie, retains uc except when buried in a complete, non-hyphenated word.

Christian Democrat is noun and adjective, as in Christian Democrat MP.

Christian name be careful of using the term in connection with non-Christians; in such cases use

forename or first name. "Given name" is an
Americanism and should be avoided.

Christie's but Christies International (no apostrophe).

Christmas day is capitalised thus.

church capitalise official names of institutions: the
Church of England, United Reformed Church, Church
Army, Methodist Church, Roman Catholic Church. But
otherwise lc, as in church and state, or buildings, as in
St John's church. Avoid "the church" meaning
institutional Christianity in general; say "the churches".
Note that the Church of Ireland, Church in Wales and
Scottish Episcopal Church are Anglican but
disestablished, the Church of Scotland is presbyterian
but established. Follow the style used here for
capitalisation.

The General Synod (lc synod at second mention)
has three houses, of bishops, clergy and laity. The
Church Commissioners have three chief officers, the
First (Second, Third) Church Estates Commissioner.
The Queen is not "head of the Church of England" but
Supreme Governor. Nor is she "head of the Church of
Scotland", who, they will tell you, is Jesus Christ.

Persons of the Trinity take an upper case pronoun:
God is He. The qualifier "Roman" in Roman Catholic
(never abbreviated to RC) is for first mention,
afterwards just Catholic (lc "catholic" has a separate
meaning). Do not shorten Anglo-Catholic. The use of
high church is becoming obsolete; ditto low church
(now usually called Evangelical). While holy orders are
lc, use uc thus for Holy Communion, Blessed
Sacrament, Mass, requiem Mass. Use lc for ordination,
baptism, confirmation, last rites, etc. The papal
pronuncio is the ambassador in London who represents
the Holy See (for which entity "the Vatican" will usually
do), and is sufficiently described as Archbishop John

Smith. Use uc for Nonconformist and for Free Church. The United Reformed Church is composed of the former Congregationalist Church and Presbyterian Church of England. Some "Congregational" congregations remain outside the reformed group.

In Scotland, be sure to distinguish the Free Church of Scotland (the "Wee Frees") not only from the established Church of Scotland but also from the Presbyterian Church of Scotland, of which Lord Mackay is a member. There are other Scots Presbyterian groups with no less confusing titles.

TITLES

Where possible use clergy instead of clergyman or churchman, as some are female.

1 Junior clergy. Christian priests, deacons, ministers of any denomination should be "the Rev John Smith" on first mention (never the Reverend Smith or Rev Smith); on second reference, write Mr Smith, except for Roman Catholic and Orthodox clergy, for whom use Fr Smith. (Fr John Smith is also acceptable for first mention.) Not all Anglican clergy are vicars: some are rectors, some are neither. For nuns, use Sister Smith or Mother Smith, never Miss. For female clergy, the Rev Joan Smith (second mention, Mrs, Miss Smith; if marital status not known, Miss Smith). Jesuits take SJ on first mention — the Rev John Smith SJ — unless identified as such, but ignore all other order initials. For Benedictines use Fr (not Dom) Smith.

2 Senior clergy: Anglican. Archdeacons: the Archdeacon of Barchester, the Ven John Smith (second reference, Mr Smith). Cathedral deans and provosts: the Dean of Barchester, the Very Rev John Smith (Mr Smith). Rural deans are just the Rev John Smith. Canons are Canon John Smith (Canon Smith), likewise Prebendaries. Anglican archbishops and diocesan bishops in the UK: the (Archbishop) Bishop of Barchester, the (Most) Right Rev John Smith, but if a

doctor then Dr John Smith. Second reference, the bishop or Bishop Smith (never Mr), but Dr Smith if so entitled. Anglican suffragan (junior) bishops do not have dioceses, though they are named after towns. The Archbishop of Canterbury is Primate of All England; the Archbishop of York is Primate of England. As all other provinces of the Anglican Communion are headed by one primate, however, it is permissible to call Canterbury just the Church of England primate. Anglican bishops are consecrated, Roman Catholic bishops ordained.

3 Senior clergy: others. Roman Catholic archbishops and bishops in the UK: the Roman Catholic (Archbishop) Bishop of Barchester, Mgr John Smith. Second reference, as Anglican, but also Mgr Smith. (Mgr covers most Roman Catholic bishops, also some senior priests.) The Archbishop of Westminster, Cardinal John Smith, is a special case (it is not necessary to include the words Roman Catholic here, but note Roman Catholic Archdiocese of Westminster). Roman Catholic junior bishops are called auxiliary bishops, and though they technically have (semi-extinct) dioceses it is not usual to mention this. Use Mgr John Smith, auxiliary Roman Catholic bishop of Westminster. Never use suffragan in Roman Catholic context, as its meaning is different from the more common Anglican use.

The Moderator of the General Assembly of the Church of Scotland, for his year of office, is the Right Rev John McSmith, second mention Mr McSmith (NB *not* Moderator of the Church of Scotland). Retired moderators keep the title Very Rev for life.

4 Foreign prelates. In Ireland, Africa, North America, etc, say Anglican Bishop of ... (Roman Catholic Bishop of ...). In other countries the denomination may be superfluous (Archbishop of Warsaw) or supplied by context. Pope John Paul II (second reference, the Pope). In America, Episcopalian means Anglican.

civil service and civil servant are both lc, but Civil Service Commission (title). Remember rules on capitalisation: institutional titles take uc, jobs do not except where derived from some honorific function or where confusion could be caused. Thus, permanent secretary to the Treasury, private secretary to the Secretary of State, secretary of the cabinet and head of the home civil service. Where the meaning is clear, initial caps are unnecessary. See also **capitalisation**.

claim do not write that so-and-so *claimed* that such-and-such, if all you mean is that he *said* or *declared*. The word carries a suspicion of incredulity.

clichés the degeneration of a word or phrase into a cliché is a sign of a language shedding old skin in order to be renewed. A good writer knows instinctively when a word has outlived its time and should be shunned. A good writer can detect an exhausted phrase and choose a fresh one in its place. No list can help, since it would change each year. But see also **Introduction**, **adjectives**, **situation**, **vogue words**.

climate a cliché for atmosphere or opinion.

co- the prefix *co-* does not normally require a hyphen even when attached to *e* or another *o* unless confusion might result: co-operate, co-opt, co-exist. See also **hyphens**.

coal mine is two words.

Coca-Cola is spelt thus.

Cold war, the (uc C) but to be in a state of cold war (lc).

collective nouns and most corporate bodies are usually singular (the company, council, government, group, herd *is*). Avoid referring to such entities as *who*: *that* or *which* is preferable. However, this singularity is not a hard and fast rule. The best guiding principle is that if the sense directs attention to the constituents of the collective, the verb should be plural; if the sense directs attention to the collective as such, the verb should be singular. Thus, "the council was elected in March" but "the council are at sixes and sevens over rents". "The government has issued a warning ..." but "the team were tiring as the game wore on". The use of a singular verb with a collective noun is to be preferred.

Having chosen either singular or plural, be consistent throughout the sentence and all its subordinate clauses, avoiding such mistakes as: "The committee, which was appointed two years ago, presented their report yesterday". Keep to the same number for the same collective noun throughout.

Colombia is the country, Columbia the Hollywood studio, university, river, etc.

colons see **Introduction, punctuation**.

Colosseum in Rome, Coliseum in London.

Coloureds in South Africa take uc, but elsewhere the description mixed race is preferable, if mixed race is what you want to indicate. See also **blacks**.

commas see **Introduction, punctuation**.

Common Market use European Community (EC).

common sense (noun), but commonsense, commonsensical (adjective).

Commons, House of one of the two Houses of Parliament.

communiqué retains the accent.

communist be sparing in the use of cap C. It is necessary only if attachment to a Communist party is directly implied, eg, a Communist candidate, a Communist rally, the Communist mayor of Lille. But lc for communist propaganda, countries, ideology. Never use as a synonym for Marxist or left wing.

Commonwealth of Independent States see **Russia, Russians**.

community charge poll tax is acceptable usage as long as it remains a grim memory. See also **council tax**.

companies abbreviate to Co when "and Co", eg, John Brown and Co; otherwise do not abbreviate, eg, British Oxygen Company. Limited is generally unnecessary; if used abbreviate to Ltd or plc without a full point. Company is singular.

comparatively, relatively these are commonly used as general qualifiers with the sense of "fairly" or "middling". The practice should be resisted. Avoid unless there is an implied comparison or relation present. "Nine out of ten people eat oranges: comparatively few eat strawberries" is a correct use. "Comparatively few people know that Charles VIII had 12 toes" is an incorrect use.

compare use compare *to* when likenesses are the point: "... this image to a damsel fair", compare *with* for differences: "... the saint with the devil".

compass points northeast, southeast, etc. Regional phrases, if well established and in common use, take uc, eg, the North, the South East, West Country, North and South Wales, Middle West (US), Midlands, East End

(of London). West Africa, South Africa but southern
Africa. North and South Atlantic and Pacific. Eastern
Europe but the eastern seaboard of the USA. The
Middle East, but sub-Saharan Africa and south India.

comprise see **include**.

Comptroller General use uc, no hyphen.

concern avoid in most cases, eg, as synonym for a
business (or as in "to show concern", prefer "to be
concerned about ...").

Congress (US) takes uc but congressional committee,
investigation, etc are all lc; congressman (lc) is used only
of members of the lower House of Congress (House of
Representatives), not of senators. Capitalise only in
titles: Congressman John Bloggs. Also the Congress
party of India, whose official title is the Indian National
Congress.

connection not connexion.

Conservative Conservative Central Office (all uc), but
Conservative party, chairman, manifesto. Tory is an
acceptable, less formal equivalent.

Consolidated Fund takes uc.

constitution of a country, uc only when an actual
document.

conterminous not coterminous.

Continent, the (meaning mainland Europe), but
continental (lc).

contract out has no hyphen.

contractions such as don't, shan't, isn't, it's should be avoided except in quotes.

controversial should be deleted 99 times for every one appropriate use.

convener not -*or*.

convention, convocation lc except when part of official name.

cooling tower pictures of cooling towers should not be used to illustrate stories about air pollution. What emerges from them is water vapour, which is harmless. Chimneys with real smoke are acceptable.

co-operation use hyphen; but uncooperative. See also **hyphens**.

council lc in local authority names. Avoid councillor as title in front of a name; use Mr Smith, a councillor.

council tax replacement for community charge (poll tax).

counties spell out names except in lists; no -*shire* with Devon, Dorset, Somerset. Irish county names are preceded by county, shortened to co. (lc, with point) Donegal.

county court takes lc unless preceded by name, as in Devon County Court. See also **courts**.

coup is a brilliant stroke. A coup d'etat (noun) is an illegal seizure of power, for which coup is an accepted abbreviation in context.

court martial plural courts martial, Courts-Martial

Appeal court; to court-martial (verb).

Court of St James's takes uc, apostrophe *s*.

Court of Session Edinburgh not Sessions.

courts a world where accuracy is particularly important. Follow carefully the style used here for capitalisation, hyphenation, etc.

THE COURTS

1 Criminal cases. The vast majority of less serious criminal cases are dealt with by magistrates' courts. They are presided over by lay justices or magistrates. In a few of the busiest magistrates' courts there are full-time paid magistrates, or stipendiaries. The more serious criminal cases are heard in the crown court. The most famous of these, in the City of London, is the Central Criminal Court, which is in a street called the Old Bailey. "Old Bailey" is an acceptable term for the court itself.

2 Civil cases. These are heard in magistrates' courts and county courts, the more serious in the High Court. The High Court has three parts or divisions for different kinds of cases, although there is some overlap: the Queen's Bench, Chancery and Family divisions. They have their base at the Royal Courts of Justice in the Strand. The divisional court of the Queen's Bench division can quash decisions by magistrates' courts and hear appeals from lower courts on points of law. It is also the main court for reviewing administrative decisions by governmental bodies or local authorities.

3 Court of Appeal. Do not say appeal court. There is no need to say "three judges in the Court of Appeal heard ..."; three is the normal number.

4 Scottish courts. Court of Session, Edinburgh (civil actions); High Court of Judiciary; Senator of the College

of Justice; Lord Justice-General, Lord Justice-clerk; sheriff court (not sheriff's); the Procurator Fiscal is the Crown prosecutor in Scotland; pursuer (English plaintiff); defender (defendant); libel (writ containing pursuer's allegations).

COURT REPORTING

In general, courts and the people in them take lc, for instance "the court". So do judge, recorder, chairman, county court, stipendiary, magistrate, etc. But Recorder of Cardiff, the West London Magistrate and so on. Bench takes uc only when referring to the judges as a group, for example when talking about the judicial Bench as opposed to the Bar of an Inn (see below).

1 Criminal cases. Lawyers in criminal cases appear "for the prosecution" or "for the defence". Avoid "defending" and "prosecuting". Defendants usually "admit" or "deny" offences, avoiding both the clumsy word "pleaded" and the danger of the "not" in "not guilty" getting lost. The law says that juveniles who appear in an adult court may be named, although *The Times* generally does not. Seek editorial authority before letting the name of anybody under 17 appear in any context in any court case. Do not report the details of sex offences against children and avoid letting reports of sex trials become surreptitious pornography. In long-running court cases, say when the case continues. If a case has ended, always give the verdict. Defendants on trial receive normal title style until they are convicted.

2 Civil cases. The parties in civil cases are the plaintiff and the defendant. Use "counsel for Mr X" in preference to "counsel for the plaintiff/defendant", once it is clear who is who.

3 Appeals. In appeals, the defendant becomes the appellant. But again, normally refer to individuals — "counsel for ABC Public Relations", or "counsel for Mrs Jones" — to avoid frequent use of "the appellant". The respondent is usually the Crown. Use "counsel for the Crown".

4 Judges. In the *magistrates' courts* the bench is always lc. The preferred style is "the magistrates at Bristol" or "the Bristol magistrates", rather than "Bristol magistrates' court". If there is more than one bench sitting in the same town it must be correctly identified, making clear whether it is a borough or a county magistrates' bench.

At the *Central Criminal Court* the Recorder of London is usually referred to as "the Recorder", without "of London"; and similarly the Common Sergeant.

The *district judge* is a new kind of judge, replacing the old county court registrar, and is referred to as District Judge Brown.

A *circuit judge* sits either in the crown court or in the county court and should be referred to as Judge Bean, not Judge Roy Bean, unless there are two with the same surname. If QCs, they retain the initials. They can also be referred to as His (or Her) Honour and in court are addressed as Your Honour. Note that in the Central Criminal Court, although the judges are ordinary circuit judges, they are also called My Lord. As a rule, in a court context, use Judge Bean QC rather than His Honour. Retired circuit judges retain His Honour, but drop the title Judge.

High Court judge Mr (or Mrs/Miss) Justice Bean, all the way through. These judges have a knighthood and may also be described as Sir John (or Dame Margaret) Bean. In court they are addressed as My Lord or My Lady. In general use Mr Justice Bean in a court context.

Court of Appeal A judge is a Lord Justice of Appeal. Use Lord Justice and surname all the way through or, out of court, Sir John Bean. They are addressed as My Lord or My Lady.

House of Lords (or law lords). These are the most senior judges. They are the Lords of Appeal in

Ordinary. Describe them as Lord Bean, in or out of
court. When writing about a House of Lords judgment
say: "the House of Lords ruled" or "the law lords ruled".

5 Other terms. *Legal officers* When there is only one,
capitals are used, as in Official Solicitor, Treasury
Solicitor, Senior Official Referee, Senior Official
Receiver. There are several official referees and official
receivers. They take lc.

Names of counsel As with other stories, one
Christian (first) name is to be preferred to one initial;
two or more initials are acceptable. When possible give
the name of a barrister or solicitor in the form he or
she uses. When in doubt, use the initials of the names
given in one of the legal directories (or first name if
there is only one). Do not use Messrs for firms of
solicitors; individual solicitors acting alone take
Mr/Mrs/Miss. Firms of solicitors are always firms,
never companies.

Affidavits An affidavit read in a civil court should be
so described, and not called "written evidence". Under
the Criminal Justice Act 1967, "written statements" are
permissible in certain criminal proceedings.

Acts Statutes are officially printed without a comma
between the title and the year (as in Criminal Justice Act
1967). An act always takes uc when its title is being
used, but bill, statute, order, regulation, measure (except
Church of England Measure) take lc. Note that Part I,
etc, of the (Finance) Act takes uc, but article, paragraph,
clause, section and schedule are all lc.

Cases In the Law Report cases cited go in italics, eg,
Conway v. Rimmer and in *Conway*'s case. In news
stories roman type should be retained.

Inns of Court The four Inns always take uc, even
when Inn is used on its own, like Bar. Also Bench and
Masters of the Bench, but benchers. The order of
precedence among the Inns is: Lincoln's Inn, Inner
Temple, Middle Temple, Gray's Inn.

At an *inquest* a coroner takes lc: the Westminster

coroner. Juries return the verdict, a coroner records it.
Pathologists should not be called Home Office
pathologists unless they are attached to a government
forensic laboratory. There is none in the Metropolitan
Police district, pathologists here and in most places are
private consultants, paid by the coroner. When in doubt
use "pathologist" only. Scientists attached to Scotland
Yard or to forensic laboratories elsewhere should be
described as forensic scientists, not forensic experts.
There are no coroner's inquests in Scotland; violent or
unexplained deaths are reported to the Procurator
Fiscal, who may hold an enquiry. See also **forensic**.

Latin words, etc Latin and French words and
phrases go in roman lc, eg, mandamus, certiorari,
habeas corpus, etc. Maxims take italics, eg, *caveat
emptor*.

Creole a person born in the West Indies or Latin
America whose ancestry is wholly or partly European.
The word does not imply mixed race.

crescendo means getting louder. Nothing "rises to a
crescendo". The plural is crescendos. See also **musical
nomenclature**.

crime report crime statistics with great care as they are
known to be a factor increasing public fear. The most
authoritative figures for Britain come from the Home
Office British Crime Survey, based on random sample
polling. Figures from the police are quite different,
based on reports to police stations. The latter should
always be given with the qualification, "reported to the
police". Headlines on police crime stories should not say
"crime soars ..." except with some qualification or
attribution. Be extremely careful about comparisons
between crime figures, especially international ones. If
provided by the police they are likely to be unreliable
over time, as reporting practice varies widely between

police forces, and indeed between police stations.

crisis this most abused word is a technical term for a process reaching a turning point. It therefore never deepens, grows, mounts or worsens, and is certainly never a continuous state, as in housing crisis or hostage crisis. Economics are never "in crisis". "Crisis situation" is so meaningless as to be banned. The adjective *critical* is subject to the same caveats. See also **situation**.

criterion plural, criteria.

cross benches two words but crossbenchers, crossbench opinion.

Crown (in constitutional sense) is capitalised, as in Crown property, the Crown representative. See also **royal**, **titles**.

Crown Estate Commissioners not Estates.

Cruft's Show is spelt thus.

crunch avoid, as in "reaches crunch point".

cupfuls spoonfuls (not cupsful, etc).

currencies should always be converted into sterling on news/feature pages. In the business section, US dollars need not be converted, nor French francs and deutschmarks except where necessary to assist the flow of the story.

current the use of *present* is preferable, or reconstruct the sentence using the admirable *now*. Most temporal references are superfluous. Rather than write "the current cabinet" or "the cabinet currently [now] in power", better write just "the cabinet" and get on with the story. See also **present**.

Custom House (the headquarters building) takes uc.

Customs (and Excise), uc for the organisation, lc for customs officer, customs post.

Czech refers to the larger part of Czechoslovakia and is distinct from Slovak. The adjective is Czechoslovak. Technically there is no Czechoslovak language, so specify Czech or Slovak if you can.

D

Dail Eireann the lower house of the Irish parliament, usually referred to as the Dail.

damp not dampen.

Dark Ages takes uc, but use the term with caution. The period following the fall of the Roman empire is no longer considered wholly obscure and barbaric.

dashes see **punctuation**.

data strictly plural, but common usage makes it a singular collective noun when what is referred to is clearly singular: "There is no data to support that conclusion."

dates Monday, April 15, 1985, but April 1985 (no commas). When citing periods of years use minimum figures: 1904-7, 1920-1, 1927-35 (but, following the spoken word, not in the tens: thus 1914-18). Do not write, "He reigned between 1926-35". Make it either "from 1926 to 1935" or "between 1926 and 1935".

Common usage says that the last decade ended on
December 31, 1989, and the century ends on
December 31, 1999.

day is lc in Christmas day, Easter day, New Year's day,
Thanksgiving day.

deal avoid "a good/great deal" as a synonym for *much*.
See also **great**.

deal with avoid. It is usually meaningless and
superfluous.

dean do not use this Americanism for doyen.

debatable avoid as synonym of dubious.

decades use either the 1960s or the sixties (not the
'60s).

decibel a measure of the intensity level of a sound (the
rate at which energy falls on a given area) relative to a
standard intensity; it is not a measure of noise, ie, of
sensation. The noise level involves not only the intensity
level of the sound but also the sensitivity of the ear at
the frequency in question. The unit of noise is the phon.
"I cannot stand the decibels" should read "... the noise".

decimals do not mix decimals with fractions in same
story. Obey the "rule of three", that only three numbers
can be comprehended before rounding up or down.
Round down below 0.5 and up to the next unit for 0.5
and above. See also **numbers**.

decimate means to kill (roughly) one in ten. Custom
has hallowed its extension to "kill a large proportion
of". But further extension is a cliché.

48

decorations see **honours**.

definite avoid using with "decision", which should always be definite.

definite article should not be omitted for brevity or to avoid monotony at the start of consecutive paragraphs, as in "Main aim of the exercise is ...". It should be left out where it serves no purpose, eg, "of (the) 480 pupils who took the test" when that is the first mention of the number.

degrees (weather): centigrade/celsius in news stories, as 16°C (or minus 16°C) but continue to give fahrenheit equivalent.

demi- means half, used only in demigod, demijohn, demimonde and demitasse. See also **hemi-, semi-**.

demo use demonstration.

Democratic party (US) not Democrat party. The adjective is Democrat in other uses, as in "the Democrat spokesman".

deny see **rebut**.

departments of government capitalised for formal title, eg, Department of the Environment, but otherwise lc: the employment department. Remember that some departments are still content to be humble, such as the Ministry of Defence. See also **capitalisation**.

dependant (noun) but dependent (adjective).

despite the fact that means "although". But despite is a synonym of "in spite of".

deutschmark use "the mark" not "the D-mark". With figures, DM (eg, DM42). See also **currencies**.

differ use differ from, different from, not *than* or *to*. "He behaved different than his sister" is an Americanism that should not be copied.

dilate makes dilatation, not dilation.

diphtheria not diptheria.

diphthong not dipthong.

diplomat for people in the foreign services, not diplomatist.

diplomatic terms avoid unless reporting their use elsewhere. Use roman for aide memoire, demarche, etc. Use English words wherever possible.

disabled beware of offensive metaphors. Do not use medical terms for metaphors. Also avoid the new and often patronising American euphemisms, such as "disadvantaged" and "physically challenged". But common usage changes here, so be sensitive. See also **medical terms, "political correctness"**.

discomfit a strong word whose first meaning is to defeat or utterly to rout, but by extension might mean thoroughly to embarrass. It has no connection with *discomfort* in spite of the similarity of sound. "The noise of drilling went on all day, to the discomfiture of the residents" is a misuse.

discreet means tactful, circumspect: "I am afraid I was not very discreet". *Discrete* means individually distinct: "There are four discrete sound sources from a quadraphonic system". The noun from discreet is discretion, from discrete is discreteness.

disinterested means impartial, unbiased, and is not the same as uninterested. Disinterest is thus not the noun from uninterested. Use "lack of interest".

dispatch not despatch.

dissociate not disassociate.

do one of the finest verbs in the English language, for which journalists unaccountably seek ugly euphemisms such as execute, operate, carry out, etc. But for *don't* see **apostrophe**.

docklands lc except in east London, where Docklands is common usage.

doctor some style guides deny the title Dr (no full point) to all but medical practitioners. If somebody has a doctorate from a reputable institution and wishes to be known as Dr Smith, they should be so titled (see also **appellations**). Many medical "doctors" are not practitioners but teach or research. To strip distinguished scholars of their academic titles is offensive.

Dominican Republic neighbour to Haiti; Dominica is quite different and is one of the Windward Islands. Both are sovereign states.

donate use give or present.

Dostoevsky is spelt thus.

drachmas not drachmae.

draftsman (legal) but draughtsman (art, design).

dramatic irony is when an audience or reader perceives a point that the characters concerned appear not to perceive. Do not use for any misapprehension.

dreamt not dreamed.

drier is a comparative adjective; dryer is a noun.

drop a bombshell never do so.

drowned use to mean that a person suffocated in water or other liquid; use "was drowned" to indicate that another person caused death by holding the victim's head under water.

drugs covers legal and illegal substances that alter the physiological state of living organisms. Most people use drugs, only some people abuse them. Abuse applies to excessive use of drugs that are in some sense addictive, whether legal or illegal. Narcotics are drugs that have a depressant effect on the brain, but the term is commonly applied to a wide range of depressants and stimulants. Again, use is not the same as abuse. Beware of the terms addiction and dependence: opinion on addiction changes regularly.

due to must not be used as the equivalent of "because of" or "owing to". *Due* is an adjective, and there must be a noun somewhere to which it refers. "His absence was due to illness" is correct; "He was absent due to illness" is wrong.

dump be careful in using as synonym of dismiss or sack.

dysentery not disentery.

E

e delete this often superfluous letter when the dictionary offers you a choice, as in judgment, acknowledgment. See also **mute e**.

each, every are constantly used with a plural pronoun in spite of being singular, eg, "each of them was busy arranging their own concerns"; "everyone must make their own arrangements". But since the plural is fast becoming a way of saying "his or her", sticking to formal grammar is pedantic. Hence, "they each have won a prize"; "everyone has what they want"; "each of us has our secrets"; but "everyone has secrets". See also **plurals**.

Earls Court no apostrophe.

earthquake see **Richter scale**.

East, the in world politics the word and its variants (Eastern Europe, Eastern block) are still distinct geopolitically and should take uc. But beware which countries you embrace by the term. See also **compass points**, **West**.

Easter day is capitalised thus.

East Germany no longer exists. Use only in an historical context. See also **Germany**.

EC correct abbreviation for European Community.

ecclesiastical words see **church**.

ecumenical not oecumenical (but respect titles).

education institutions undergraduates and postgraduates can be referred to as students, as can young people at any institution called a college. Those at school, even if called college (such as Eton and Winchester) are pupils.

1 Universities. The word university is uc when part of a title, as in the University of Oxford, but lc when used apart from the name; similarly for polytechnic and college.

Degree abbreviations should be those used by the university concerned: doctorates of literature (or letters) may be DLit, DLitt, LitD, etc. Oxford and York have DPhil instead of the more usual PhD; Oxford has DM for the commoner MD; Cambridge has ScD for doctor of science. Omit full points for degrees.

2 Colleges. These cover everything from schools to parts of universities, and must therefore be given their full title, however long. There are numerous different types of specialist colleges as well as further education colleges, tertiary colleges and colleges and institutes of higher education. Some are private, some independent, some under local authority control. The correct form for specific colleges is given in the *Education Year Book*, which lists colleges by type.

3 Schools. They too are lc except in official names. Headmaster and headmistress are one word and lc except in official titles. Some schools, eg Eton, use the form Head Master, in which case the word is separated and capitalised. St Paul's School and Manchester Grammar School call their headmaster the High Master; Dulwich, Haileybury and Marlborough call him the Master. King Edward's School, Birmingham, has a Chief Master. The correct form is given in the *Public and Preparatory Schools Year Book*, but normally use headmaster or headmistress. The colloquialism "the head" should be avoided except in headlines.

O level, A level, GCSE have no inverted commas; hyphens only when used attributively, as in O-level syllabus. Sixth form, but sixth-form college, curriculum, etc. Do not use "public school" unless strictly relevant; "independent school" is preferable. Never use the form "Highgate Public School" (or "Highgate public school"), let alone the cliché "one of the oldest ...". State schools are best described as such, especially now that some local council schools are opting out, to become "grant-assisted". Many "grammar" schools are now private institutions and many private schools are not "public". Hence the importance of describing a school's status precisely, but only if strictly necessary to a story.

educationist not -alist.

EEC use EC or European Community, not Common Market.

effectively, in effect are almost always misused. The adverb means merely that the associated verb is capable of achieving its objective, is "effective". It does not mean "almost" or "all but", for which purpose use "in effect". "In effect" also means "in the outcome", but can mean "for all practical purposes". Try "virtually", but nothing is usually better.

eg roman, no points but use a comma before it and usually after.

Eire see **Ireland**.

eisteddfod lc except when naming a particular one in full; plural eisteddfodau.

either takes a singular verb even when both subjects are embraced: "Either is good enough". Remember, either means one of two and cannot begin a sequence of

55

more than two. Beware of using the word in its ambiguous sense, when it might, or might not, imply both of two: "The law allowed him to marry either woman"; "You may drive on either side of the road".

elderly see **aged**.

embassy lc, even British embassy.

England, English beware these words when you mean British: see also **Britain**.

enquire, enquiry rather than inquire, inquiry, even in "public enquiry". But respect usage given in titles, eg Committees of Inquiry Act.

ensure means to make certain. You *insure* against risk and *assure* your life.

ERM stands for exchange-rate mechanism and is best preceded by European. European monetary union (EMU) is a different, wider concept, of which the ERM is only part. Do not confuse them.

escaped person, or escaper, not escapee (who is theoretically the one escaped from).

Eskimo plural Eskimos, but the preferred name is now Inuit or Innu. Eskimo is a word meaning "eater of raw flesh" and is regarded as an insulting name by the people themselves.

et cetera contract to etc, no full point. A comma normally precedes etc but need not follow it.

Europe includes the British Isles, so do not use Europe as equivalent to the Continent, which is an acceptable term for the continental mainland of Europe excluding

Britain. Britain does not export to Europe. It can export to the rest of Europe.

European Community (EC) use thus, not Common Market or EEC.

evacuate means to empty (make a vacuum). Buildings are evacuated; strictly speaking, people are not, except anatomically. But common usage now has children evacuated from London, the school, etc.

eventuate an ugly and unnecessary synonym for *happen*.

ever is hardly ever necessary. "Best ever" is simply "the best". Do not use such compounds as best-ever, fastest-ever, etc. Avoid "never ever" as an intensification of *never*.

ex- avoid as colloquialism for *former*, except in ex-serviceman. Say former president, etc.

exam abbreviation for examination, permissible in headlines only.

excepting do not use when "except" or "except for" is possible.

exchange-rate mechanism see **ERM**.

exclusive avoid with story of interview. Everything in *The Times* should be exclusive in some sense. If we wish to indicate some special access, we might say "in a special interview with *The Times*".

execute see **killer**.

existing the word *present* is preferable in such phrases as "the existing arrangements", "the existing rate of exchange".

extrovert not extravert.

F

façade use cedilla; see also **accents**.

face to face when a story says that two people met for talks, discussions or debate, "face to face" is otiose, and weakens the description.

face up to means no more than *face*.

fact that never use without being satisfied that it is not a circumlocution for a simpler construction. "Due to the fact that" means "because". "In spite of the fact that" means "although". "The fact that he resigned caused ..." means "His resignation caused ...". It should not be used of contentious assertions: "The fact of the matter is that the government does not support the health service" refers not to a fact but to an opinion.

fahrenheit use both celsius and fahrenheit in news stories. See also **degrees, temperature**.

falangist in Spain; phalangist in Lebanon.

fallacy means a faulty argument, not an erroneous belief.

fall-out (noun) is hyphenated.

fan prefer *supporter* for football enthusiasts, except in headlines.

Far East the term encompasses the following: China, Hong Kong, Japan, Korea, Macao, Mongolia, Taiwan. See also **Southeast Asia**.

farther is applied to literal or figurative distance and nothing else: "Nothing could be farther from the truth". Further means in addition to: "A further point ...".

Fascist (uc) for Italian party or similar political organisation elsewhere; fascist (lc) as a term of political abuse. See also **Nazi**.

fatwa not a sentence of punishment but a Muslim religious edict, carrying great weight.

Fayed Mohamed Al-Fayed and his brother Ali Fayed run Alfayed Investment Trust. These are the spellings they prefer, whatever government inspectors may say.

fellahin is plural, the singular is fellah. See also **Arab names**.

fellow, fellowship (of a college or society) is lc.

feminine designations such as authoress, aviatrix, poetess, wardress should be avoided as unnecessary. Actress is common usage, though actor embraces men and women. Avoid saying female or lady before occupations; the word woman is preferable if identity or sex is relevant. Always use just doctor or teacher if sex is not relevant.

feminism much of English usage has a masculine slant (eg, mankind, he for he/she). Try to avoid causing offence to the many women who object to this. Follow style on Ms (see **appellations**). Beware of using the masculine pronoun with occupations, as in "Call the

59

doctor/lawyer and ask him ...". While the renaming of titles can be ugly (avoid chair for chairman, except in quotes), spokeswoman is acceptable. See also **bisexual pronouns**, **sexism**.

fewer of numbers and quantities (fewer people, goals, difficulties). Use *less* of size and singular nouns (less population, scoring, difficulty). "Fewer cakes were eaten; less cake was eaten."

figures see **numbers**.

finalise is ugly as a synonym of *complete* or *finish*.

first serves as an adverb. Avoid firstly, secondly, etc, especially at the start of sentences. This practice is becoming a plague.

first person singular/plural avoid except in rare cases where personalised comment is justified. I/we are not "told" news by a source, our readers are told it by our writing. (See also **exclusive**, *The Times*.) This does not apply to colour stories, columns, features, etc.

first world war is lc. There was only one, so there is no need to distinguish it; but the Great War, uc.

flaunt to make an ostentatious or defiant display: "She flaunted her finery". To flout is to show contempt for: "He flouts the law".

floodlighting but floodlit.

flout see **flaunt**.

focused has only one *s*.

following can be a noun, "She has a large following"; a

verb, "He is following the leader"; or an adjective, "Note the following quotation". It is not a preposition: "He spoke after [not following] dinner".

foot-and-mouth disease use hyphens.

for, of both prepositions are used in official titles. Institute for ..., Institute of ... Check, and use the right one.

for-, fore- the general rule is that *e* is added only when the prefix has the meaning of *before*. Thus: forbears (refrains), forebears (ancestors); forgo (go without), forego (go before, as in "foregone conclusion").

forces the armed forces, lc.

forecast not forecasted.

Foreign and Commonwealth Office FCO, or foreign office (FO), lc, for short. See also **capitalisation**.

foreign appellations see **appellations**.

foreign places apart from exceptions listed in this guide, use the spellings in *The Times Atlas of the World*. See also **Arab names, Chinese names, place-names**.

foreign words avoid wherever there is a serviceable English one. All else is affectation and usually misspelling. Certain foreign words have everyday uses in English and have been naturalised. These should be written in roman. Where a still "alien" foreign word must be used, put it in italics. See also **italics, Latin**.

forensic means pertaining to the courts. Thus forensic as an adjective means legal, not medical. A forensic expert could just as well be a solicitor as a biochemist. Therefore use forensic medicine, forensic scientist, etc.

for ever always (two words); forever (one word) means continuously.

former, latter use only where there are two people or things. "Bill, Jill and Phil met in the former's office" should be "... met in Bill's office".

formula plural formulas, but *-ae* in mathematical contexts.

forum plural forums.

four-letter words see **obscenities**.

fractions do not mix fractions and decimals in one story, as in "One in eight people will not pay the poll tax although 29 per cent have done so to date". See also **numbers**.

franc (lc) specify Belgian, etc, if not French. If in figures, BFr40, FFr40, SwFr40. See also **currencies**.

Free Churches, Free Churchman use uc to avoid confusion.

Freemasonry, Mason use uc to avoid confusion.

free trade two words, but free-trader is hyphenated.

frescoes not frescos.

fresh water (noun), freshwater (adjective).

front bench two words, but frontbencher, frontbench power.

Fujiyama or Mt Fuji, not Mt Fujiyama.

-ful, -fuls so cupfuls, not cupsful.

further see **farther**.

G

Gaddafi, Colonel (Muammar Muhammad al-), Libyan leader. There are many current spellings. This is the best compromise between the correct but confusing Gadhdhafi and the customary but wrong Gadaffi.

gaff hook or spar; a gaffe is a blunder.

Gambia, the always use definite article.

gambit a technical term in chess meaning sacrifice in return for some supposed general advantage. Its use should be avoided in metaphor except in this sense.

gaol use jail.

gauntlet a mail glove. To throw down the gauntlet means to issue a challenge. To take up the gauntlet means to accept a challenge. To run the gauntlet is to undergo an ordeal by flogging, literally or figuratively. The word here is originally *gantlope* from the Swedish *gatlopp*, a passageway.

gay do not use as a noun meaning a homosexual, unless it appears in the official name of an organisation or in quoted matter. Use homosexual, which correctly contrasts with heterosexual. However, in a story about homosexuals and in headlines gay may be used as an adjective meaning male homosexual where the sense

63

requires a distinction with female ones, eg, between gay men and lesbians. Avoid euphemisms such as bachelor.

gender see **bisexual pronouns, sexism**.

general election always lc.

geriatric does not mean elderly, but is applied to medical treatment for the elderly (geriatric hospital, geriatric case). Never use as an abusive adjective.

Germany there is now only one. It is the Federal Republic of Germany. If referring to the region that was West Germany (also formerly the Federal Republic of Germany), use western Germany. If referring to the region that was East Germany (formerly the German Democratic Republic), use eastern Germany or the former East Germany.

gerrymander (lc), the manipulation of constituency boundaries.

ghettos do not use this word in the sense of ethnic neighbourhood. It should be used only for an area of enforced or customary segregation. Say, for example, middle-class areas or districts, not ghettos.

gibe, jibe to gibe means to taunt or sneer; to jibe means to shift direction (and is a nautical term).

gig now an acceptable term for a musical event.

gipsy see **gypsy**.

girl do not use as a synonym of woman, etc. While some women do not mind being called girls, as some men do not object to being boys, others do object. The word refers to young females who are not yet women.

girl friend two words. Avoid using the word mistress unless a measure of secrecy and subterfuge is implied. Use girl friend only for young people; otherwise woman friend or just friend where the gender is obvious. The word partner is increasingly used to describe a long-term relationship between two people who have not married. See also **boy friend**.

Girl Guides see **Scouts**.

glasnost roman, not italic, as it has now become a word in common English usage.

God is uc when referring to just one, in any religion. Pronouns referring to Him, Her, Thee, Thou, should be capitalised. Numerous gods take lc.

gold mine, gold mining two words.

goodbye one word.

good will two words but good-will (used attributively, eg, good-will mission), goodwill (of a business).

Gorbachev, Mikhail *The Times* held out long for the correct *-ov* ending but *-ev* is now common usage and should be employed. *Sic transit gloria Temporum*.

Gothic, Gothick the word Gothick distinguishes the neo-medieval revival in art, architecture and literature of the late 18th and early 19th centuries (Horace Walpole to John Nash) from the Gothic revival of the later 19th century (Pugin, etc).

government always lc, including British government, except in formal titles such as Government House and Her Majesty's Government. See also **capitalisation**.

grass-roots hyphen in both noun and adjective. This is now a cliché.

great, much great is for size, much is for quantity. Avoid great as in "Great publicity has been given to the anti-smoking campaign". Remember, all qualifiers tend to be bad style.

Great Britain see **Britain**.

greater or lesser degree the word lesser is not correct but is common usage.

Greco- not Graeco-.

green paper (governmental), lc.

grisly, grizzly grisly means horrifying, repugnant; grizzly means greyish or grizzled, or is shorthand for grizzly bear.

grottoes not grottos.

ground (reason): do not use plural unless more than one is given.

guerrilla beware of loaded terms for advocates of political violence; see also **terrorism**.

Guides see **Scouts**.

Guildhall (London), not *the* Guildhall. But since this can look odd, say London's Guildhall or the Guildhall speech.

Gulf, the Iraqis and some other Arabs dislike the term Persian Gulf. Use just the Gulf when possible, but in a continent-wide or worldwide context Persian Gulf may be necessary for clarity.

gunboat one word.

gypsy not gipsy. Capitalise references to the various groups of this migratory people, lc when used generically to mean somebody who is constantly on the move.

H

haemorrhage means heavy and potentially dangerous bleeding, not just bleeding. Beware of misuse in metaphor. "Cash haemorrhage" has become a cliché.

Hague, The both uc.

Haiti, Haitian are spelt thus.

half see **fractions, numbers**.

Hapsburg not Habsburg.

harass, harassment has only one *r*, but compare embarrass.

Haringey is a London borough, Harringay is a London neighbourhood.

Harrods no apostrophe.

Hawaiian is spelt thus.

he see **bisexual pronouns**.

headache avoid as a synonym of difficulty.

headlines typographical limitations permit a number of words that would otherwise be proscribed, such as bid (for attempt); row (clash or dispute); shock (surprise); phone (telephone). Headlines must not go beyond the facts of the text. Inverted commas should be used as little as possible, should be single and not double and should not enclose words or statements that differ from those in the report. Abbreviations in headings do not take full points even for initials indicating Christian (or first) names.

Headlines are the stamp of quality on an article. Remember the first and golden rule, the force of every headline is in the verb. If the verb is not working hard, nor will the headline. Headlines are more vulnerable to mistakes and solecisms than any text and require correspondingly greater attention. They enjoy greater stylistic flexibility than text. Normally omit titles, avoid definite and indefinite articles. Avoid numbers, initials and capitals. But above all, avoid headline clichés: get under way, set to go, and hyperboles such as crisis, chaos, crash, snub, slam, etc.

headmaster, headmistress one word, lc. See also **education institutions**.

head teacher two words.

heavenly bodies capitalise the proper names of planets, stars, constellations, etc: Venus, Arcturus, the Plough, Aries. For comets, capitalise only the proper-noun element of the name: Halley's comet. Sun takes uc, but moon is generally lc. Nouns and adjectives from the proper names of planets and other heavenly bodies take lc: jovian, lunar, martian, solar, venusian.

help do not omit *to* before a following verb. People help others *to* do things; they do not help them do things.

hemi- prefix meaning half, used with words of Greek origin. See also **demi-** and **semi-**.

Hezbollah (Party of God) in Iran and Lebanon, break after Hezb-.

hiccup, hiccupped not hiccough.

high acceptable usage as a noun. But beware of "all-time high", "hits new high", and other clichés.

High Court see **courts**.

high-tech (adjective), but spell out high technology first time; hi-tech is acceptable in headlines.

hijack no hyphen.

hippy, hippies as old-fashioned as beatnik. The rebels against convention who travel round the summer festivals now call themselves travellers.

historic, historical overused and often incorrect adjectives. Historical can refer only to past history, being the adjective from history. Historic can refer to a contemporary event likely to be of long-term significance. Avoid with every passing summit. A historic building is strictly one of historical interest, though is now widely regarded as merely old.

hit should be avoided in the sense of affected, as in "Home-owners hit by interest rate rise". Hit as a synonym of attack or criticise should be used only when necessary in headlines.

HIV is a virus, not a disease. It may or may not lead to Aids, and we should be most careful not to imply that it always does. See also **Aids**.

HMSO prefer the Stationery Office (uc).

Holland preferable to The Netherlands.

home should not be a synonym of house, whatever estate agents may pretend.

Home Office is uc, but home secretary lc. See also **capitalisation**.

homogeneous not homogenous, but the verb is homogenise.

homosexual see **gay**.

Hong Kong but Hongkong & Shanghai Banking Corporation.

honours and decorations normally omit after names, except CH, FRS, GC, MP, OM, QC, RA, VC. People are created or appointed CBE, OBE, etc. They do not receive or get the awards. At investitures, they receive the insignia, not the award. See also **titles**.

Hoover is a trade name, so uc. Use vacuum as a verb.

hopefully controversial even in *The Times* office, but so widely spoken by all and sundry, in the sense of "I hope that", as to be common usage. It is an adverb known as an "attitudinal disjunct", like luckily and regrettably, and is best avoided but not banned. Some maintain that, with its adjoining verb, it constitutes a new grammatical construction of its own, the "future aspirational".

House of Commons/Lords/Representatives see **capitalisation**.

however a strong conjunction of contrast, requiring commas for its protection. Do not overuse in this sense, especially at the start of paragraphs.

Husain, King (of Jordan), but Hussein, President Saddam (of Iraq). The different spellings of the identical names are common usage, and incidentally avoid confusion.

hyperbole avoid it, especially in familiar adjectives nowadays devoid of force: radical change, far-reaching reform, historic meeting. Yesterday's hyperbole is tomorrow's cliché.

hyphens avoid hyphens unless the meaning requires them. They should be used to separate amalgamated words that look odd without them (usually because of the same adjacent letter) but not words that can easily be run together. With prefixes: prearrange, postwar, antitrust, nonexistent, nonconformist, but pre-empt, co-operate, re-establish. Keep ordinary words apart unless sense requires them to be run together. Thus air force but aircraft carrier, coal miner but steelworker, policy document but policymaking. Even adjectives formed from two or more words need not take a hyphen unless sense demands it: deputy general secretary but private-sector business. Sense and appearance are more important than rules.

In double-barrelled titles such as attorney general, director-general, the style should be that designated by the authority that created the office.

Never use dangling hyphens in constructions such as "whole- or part-time employment". But this does not apply to prefixes, "pre- and postwar". An adverb should not be joined by a hyphen to a following adjective or participle unless there is a real risk of ambiguity. Thus, a well bred horse, a clearly labelled bottle, but the best-known painting.

I

I see **first person singular**.

ie roman no points, but use a comma either side.

imagery beware of excessive imagery in journalism. See **adjectives**.

impresario has one *s*.

in addition to there are preferable alternatives: "as well as" or "besides".

incident a colourless word, used too often.

include use in a series when the items that follow are only part of the total: "The price includes breakfast." Use *comprise* when a full list of individual elements is given.

incomunicado has one *m*.

index plural indices, but indexes for books.

Indian beware too general a use of this word. It refers to natives of India. American Indians should be so called, unless the context is clear. Others of Asian origin are Asians. See also **blacks**.

inevitable often misused for customary, usual or predictable.

in fact like "of course", the phrase is grossly overworked in newspaper stories. It can usually be omitted unless particular emphasis is required.

initial prefer *first*.

initials unless an abbreviation or acronym is so familiar that the full form is rarely used (BBC, Nato, TUC), spell it out. If it occurs more than once, spell it out the first time, putting the abbreviation in parentheses, and use the abbreviation thereafter. That said, avoid alphabet soups. Refer to "the ministry" or "the organisation" where appropriate. Where institutions are known by their initials, these must be capitalised, but avoid points between them: EC, MP, OECD, RSPB, UN. Where the initials are pronounced, use upper and lower case: Gatt, Mori, Nato, Unesco. Use short forms for weights and measures: gdp, km, lb and mph (always singular and always lc; see also **scientific measurements**). But spell out miles and pages. Where initials are used with a name, use full points between them, but normally use Christian (or first) and surnames in full. See also **appellations**.

injure, injury implies something rather more serious than *hurt*. A kick in a game may hurt without injuring. The word hurt, as applied to accident victims, should be used only in headlines. Injured or sick people should not be described as satisfactory. It is their condition that is satisfactory, critical, etc.

innocent beware of this word, especially before the word victim. "Innocent victim of a terrorist attack" implies that other victims might be guilty. Innocent means "not guilty" and should not be used with "children", or of victims of disease, war or in other non-legal contexts.

innocuous is spelt thus.

Inns of Court see **courts**.

73

inoculate has only one *n*.

inquire see **enquire**.

insignia is plural.

in so far as avoid, but if used, space out.

install but instalment.

instil has only one *l*.

institute tedious verb for begin, build, do or set up.

insure against risk. You *assure* your life; to *ensure* is to make certain.

intelligentsia is spelt thus.

intensive is not a synonym of intense or extreme but the opposite of extensive. It means concentrated, as in "intensive care".

interdependence has no hyphen.

interesting one of the least interesting words in the language. Boring, dreary, worse when propped up with *very*, it should be avoided.

inverted commas see **quotation marks**.

Iran (not Persia) for the modern state.

Ireland the two parts should be called the Republic of Ireland or the Irish Republic, and Northern Ireland. Eire (which is the Irish word for Ireland) should be used only in headlines. Ulster (to which one party takes exception since a part of the old province is in the

Republic) is allowed as a variant of Northern Ireland. The Six Counties (to which the other party takes even more exception) should not be used. "The province" is useful for later references. The government in Dublin is the Irish government. Do not refer to it as the Dublin government. There is no government of Northern Ireland, which is still ruled directly from Westminster: "The British authorities in Belfast" or "ministers in Belfast" would be appropriate. See also **Northern Ireland**.

Irish use Irish spelling for Irish words where appropriate.

Irish Republican Army IRA is an acceptable abbreviation at first mention. The active IRA in Ulster is "provisional", but IRA is common usage for PIRA. The organisation is well known and needs no descriptive or derogatory epithet in *The Times*. It is paramilitary and illegal but its status as such should not be distinguished from that of other similar groups in Ulster. See also **Loyalist**, **Northern Ireland**, **terrorism**, **Ulster Defence Regiment**.

Iron Curtain no longer exists, but how it went is moot. It was not drawn or raised or lowered, so perhaps it has just "gone".

ironic beware of misuse and avoid sentences starting "Ironically". It does not mean strange or paradoxical, let alone noteworthy.

-ise, -isation avoid the *z* construction in almost all cases. This is volcanic ground, with common usage straining the crust of classical etymology. This guidance is a revision of the Greek zeta root ending in the direction of a Latin ending and common usage: apologise, organise, emphasise, televise, circumcise. The only truly awkward result is capsize, which should be left in its Grecian peace.

Islam is the religion of the Muslims. Islamic is interchangeable with Muslim as the adjective from Islam. Normally use Islamic with religion, Muslim with adherent, architecture, politics, etc.

Israeli is a native of Israel. Israelite refers to ancient Israel.

issue means outcome, not controversy. It is a sloppy word, especially when fixed to "policy". Avoid sentences starting "The issue is ...". Nine times out of ten the word can be dropped: "They debated the issue of housing" means "They debated housing".

it remember Cobbett: "Never put an *it* on paper without thinking well what you are about." Both Fowler and Gowers describe the word as "deeply troublesome". The word seduces writers to sloppy sentence construction. Always try to rewrite, and concede defeat only in extremis. Nothing looks worse than a paragraph full of *its*. A paragraph opening with one looks dreadful. *It* is a lifeless word and is best confined to referrals back to a noun within the same sentence or the immediately preceding one. Beware of more than one *it* referring to different nouns in one sentence.

Almost every use of the word can be avoided by reconstructing a sentence and clarifying its meaning. But "It is odd that ..." is an acceptable construction.

italics should usually be avoided. Put most foreign words in italics, but these words should be used sparingly. Where a foreign word has entered common English usage, italics can be abandoned. Err on the side of roman: in extremis, hors d'oeuvre, Zeitgeist. Italics are appropriate to stress a word under discussion, in preference to the uglier practice of putting that word inside quotation marks. Italics are also to be used for the titles of newspapers, books, films, plays, and larger musical works. Poetry should not be italicised. But use discretion: italics may be needed to help reading and avoid confusion (eg, the use of *one*). See also **foreign words, musical nomenclature, one, quotation marks**.

ITV use independent television; see also **television**.

-ize see **-ise**.

J

Jacuzzi is a trade name, so takes uc.

jail, jailer not gaol, etc.

jargon the primary meaning is the specialised vocabulary and idioms of a particular occupational group. In general, avoid it. When appropriate in a special context, give an explanation of words likely to be unfamiliar to most readers.

jeweller, jewellery not jewelry (which is the American spelling).

jihad holy war, use roman, not italic, as it has now become a word in common English usage.

journalese is the bogus jargon of journalists, prevalent in headlines, where words that nobody else uses creep in for reasons of brevity or impact. Journalese is to be avoided at all times. The language of *The Times*, even in headlines, is the language of the intelligent English-speaking world. See also **headlines**.

jubilee strictly means a fiftieth anniversary. This did not stop Queen Victoria having golden and diamond ones; as a result jubilee now means a periodic celebration, especially of royalty.

judgment only one *e* (not judgement).

junior as in John Smith Jr (uc, no comma or full point). Avoid the Americanism Jnr.

juvenile court lc; see also **courts**.

K

k avoid for 1,000, except in quotes.

Kafir an offensive word for black African. But Kaffirs (stocks).

Katharine always check spelling (Catherine, Katherine).

kerosene American for paraffin.

Khmer Rouge the name of a Cambodian faction. A Khmer is a Cambodian.

killer a neutral word, but where applicable, the more deadpan *murderer* is preferable. An assassin is the murderer of a statesman or senior politician from a political motive. It should not be used of other celebrities. The word slay is biblical and is not to be used in headlines. Avoid all words that glamorise or euphemise murder. Execution is a judicial killing after due process of law under state authority.

King's College London has an apostrophe but no

comma.

King's Cross the station is spelt thus.

Kingston upon Thames has no hyphens.

knowledgeable retains the *e* after *g*.

Koran see **Islam**.

Ku-Klux-Klan all uc, hyphens.

L

Ladbroke's the betting shop, but Ladbroke plc.

lady, ladies regarded as genteel, opposite of gentlemen. Use woman, women. See also **feminine designations**, **sexism**.

laisser faire roman, not italic.

Lake District do not write the word Lake when the name contains its equivalent. Thus, Windermere and Derwent Water, but Lake Bassenthwaite.

Land-Rover takes uc and hyphen.

Land's End is spelt thus.

landslide (political) and landslip (earth).

last take care not to use as a synonym of latest. "The last announcement was made at midnight" leaves the reader wondering whether this was the final announcement, or whether others follow. Do not use "last few days" when "past few days" is meant.

Latin except in law reports, always seek to write English. Phrases such as *ne plus ultra, nil desperandum, si monumentum requiris,* tend to read as pretentious and have valid English equivalents. Some phrases are clearly common usage, such as quid pro quo and QED. A good test is that a phrase should be well enough known to be printed in roman. See also **italics**.

latitude, longitude are given thus: 45° 32'N, 40° 17'W.

law see **courts**.

layout is one word.

Leader of the House is a formal title and takes uc, leader of the Opposition is a descriptive one and takes lc, as does the leader of the Conservative party, etc.

leakage is not a dignified substitute for leak. It means the amount or rate of loss caused by a leak.

lean, leap make leant and leapt, which *The Times* prefers to leaned and leaped.

Lea River but Lee Valley Regional Park Authority, Lee Valley Water plc.

learned (adjective) but learnt (all verbal uses).

Lebanon not *the* Lebanon.

left, the (political): the left wing, left-wing contenders, leftwingers, all lc.

legionella, listeria, salmonella are all bacteria, not viruses.

legionnaires' disease is lc, plural.

Legion of Honour use English form, uc.

leper do not use as a metaphor or as a term of abuse.

less in quantity, fewer in number. See also **fewer, great**.

lesser opposite to greater. Do not use instead of less: "lesser educated people" is wrong for "less educated".

leukaemia is spelt thus.

liaison is often used where the word link would be better. The ubiquitous back formation liaise should be avoided as a genteel synonym of meet or talk.

Liberal Democrat is a noun, Liberal Democratic party, MPs, etc. Democrats for short; Lib Dems only in headlines.

licence (noun) but license (verb) and licensed.

lifebelt, lifeboat are one word, but Royal National Life-boat Institution (RNLI).

lifestyle the phrase "style of living" is preferable, and never "live a lifestyle".

lighted (past participle) and lit (past tense). But the words are nowadays interchangeable.

likable has only one *e*.

like a word of comparison, not inclusion, and should not be used instead of "such as". However frequent this mistake — "stars like Olivier walked this stage" — it is still a mistake. Avoid such forms as "It looks like he's scoring" or "It looks like a goal" when you mean he is about to score. The alternative is: "It looks as if he is going to score".

literally best avoided as an adverb of emphasis, as in "There were literally thousands of people there". When mixed into a metaphor the result is absurd: "He literally exploded with anger".

livid is not a synonym for red. It means blue-black. If a person becomes livid with rage, his face cannot become red or white, but may be leaden. However, the word is now common usage for angry.

Lloyds Bank no apostrophe.

Lloyd's of London the formal name for the insurance market based in Lime Street in the City of London. Lloyd's is not a single insurance company.

Lloyd's insurance informal version of Lloyd's of London.

Lloyd's List a daily newspaper covering insurance, shipping and general finance produced and owned by Lloyd's of London Press, the publications department of Lloyd's of London.

Lloyd's Register of Shipping a classification society that sets out minimum international standards of construction for ships, boilers and industrial plant. It is not a regulatory body and has no direct link with Lloyd's of London, although Lloyd's of London is represented on Lloyd's Register's ruling committee. An annual register of all international merchant shipping over 100 tonnes is published by Lloyd's Register of Shipping. "A1 at Lloyd's" is the top classification for ships from Lloyd's Register.

loan is a noun; the verb is lend. For "The picture is on loan ...", prefer "... has been lent ...".

loathe (verb) and loath (adjective), not *loth*.

local often used unnecessarily, as in "local residents".

local government it is important to follow style for names, capitalisation, etc.

Councils The word council is lc except when full title is given, eg, Watford Borough Council, Manchester City Council, Newtown District Council. After the first mention, if it is necessary to distinguish between a number of councils referred to in a story, such a form as Watford council, the city council, Newtown district council may be used. The names of all committees take lc or we shall drown in alphabet soup: Newtown council highways, parks and gardens committee.

By custom "the Lord Mayor" by itself refers to the Lord Mayor of London. All other lord mayors and all mayors are lc unless the title is given in full, eg, the Lord Mayor of Manchester, the Mayor of Bolton.

Councillor is a job as well as a title, but its titular use is cumbersome. Refer to John Jones, or to Mr Jones, a councillor, where the status is relevant to a story.

Local government officials, eg, borough surveyor, borough treasurer, town clerk, all take lc. The headline abbreviation for medical officer of health is MoH. The local guildhall takes lc, as do town hall, city hall, city chambers. In the City of London, Guildhall does not take the definite article and is always uc.

Distinguish between Authority as part of an official title (eg, Port of London Authority) and authority, lc, as a description of a function (eg, Hampshire police authority).

London The local council for the City of London is called the Court of Common Council. The chairman of the City lands committee is called the Chief Commoner. Members of the Common Council are called common councilmen (not councillors). Aldermen who are not peers, dames, baronets or knights are styled "Mr/Madam Alderman Evelyn Smith". Each alderman has a deputy, who is styled "Mr/Madam Deputy Evelyn Jones". In formal contexts use the style "Lord Mayor, Aldermen and Sheriffs". In normal usage aldermen and sheriffs take lc. Not all guilds are livery companies, but most are. The formal style "Worshipful Company of Goldsmiths" should not be used except when quoting an official statement. Usage is "the Goldsmiths' Company", capitalised to avoid confusion. Livery halls do not take the definite article, eg, "Drapers' Hall", not "the Drapers' Hall".

There are two sorts of freedom of the City of London: the honorary freedom, conferred only on distinguished people for special services to the City or nation; and the ordinary freedom, which can be bought or acquired by citizens with certain qualifications. There are several thousand freemen of the City of London; to describe a man or woman as a freeman of the City as if it were a personal honour or distinction is misleading, and should be avoided.

London borough of ... takes lc. The London County Council and the Greater London Council no longer exist. The London Boroughs Association and the Association of London Authorities are unofficial groups. The only official London-wide planning body is the London Planning Advisory Committee.

lord, lady see **peers**, **titles**.

Lord Advocate do not add "for Scotland".

Lord Chancellor is always uc.

Lord Chief Justice is always uc.

lord(s) lieutenant has no hyphen.

Lord's cricket ground has an apostrophe.

Lords, House of takes uc, but lords and ladies, live like a lord, etc, all lc.

lords justices both words take the plural.

lorry not truck.

loudhailer, loudspeaker both one word.

lovable has only one *e*.

lover see **boy friend**.

Loyalist (Northern Ireland): beware the use as a synonym of Protestant or Unionist. It is in common use as an epithet for Unionist paramilitaries, in which case always give it uc. See also **Northern Ireland**.

Ltd can be dropped from company names unless it aids comprehension.

Luxembourg is spelt thus.

-lyse write analyse, paralyse, rather than use *z*. See also **-ise**, **-zed**.

M

M1 not "M1 motorway". See also **roads**.

Mac, Mc check spelling of all such prefixes in *Who's Who*, etc, before use. Alphabetise all variants as if spelt Mac.

McDonald's hamburger chain is spelt thus.

machinegun, sub-machine gun a machinegun (one word) is a large weapon mounted on a stand and is rarely used in crime. A sub-machine gun (two words) is an automatic or semi-automatic weapon carried by one person.

macho avoid as adjective. The noun machismo is acceptable.

macintosh the rainproof coat has no *k*.

Magdalen College Oxford but Magdalene College, Cambridge.

Maghreb see **Middle East**.

magistrates' courts not police courts. See also **courts**.

Magna Carta not *the* Magna Carta.

maisonette is set in roman type.

major appears too often in place of big, chief, important or main and should be avoided except as a comparative. "Very major" and "more major" are ungrammatical.

majority of nearly always an unnecessary substitute for most of, eg, "the majority of the population" for "most of the population".

man, mankind these words offend many women and should normally be contrastable with woman, womankind. The words humans, humanity, people are preferable. See also **feminine designations, sexism**.

manifestos not -*oes*.

manuscript(s) write out when part of a sentence, abbreviate when quotation from a catalogue, eg, Harleian MSS.

marathon a cliché for unexpectedly prolonged events or exercises, as in marathon session. Acceptable only in extreme cases.

Marks & Spencer always use ampersand.

marquess not marquis, except for foreign titles.

Marxist takes uc as noun and adjective referring to a follower of Karl Marx. Use only where the reference is precise, or claimed by the subject. Do not use as variant of communist, let alone left wing. A student of Marx or Marxism, not necessarily an ideological follower, is nowadays often a Marxian. This is a useful distinction.

Master of the Queen's Music takes uc and is now spelt thus.

Master of the Rolls takes uc.

Matabele singular and plural: a Matabele is a member of the Matabele people. The Matabele are now officially the Ndebele.

materialise best saved for its proper and rare spiritualist use, since it is an ugly and unnecessary substitute for appear, come about, happen. A metaphorical use is just permissible of an event "failing to materialise" despite concentrated effort on all sides.

mathematics spell out in full; maths only in headlines.

maybe prefer the word perhaps.

Mayday (SOS), but May Day (holiday).

Mayfair but May Fair Hotel.

mayor uc only before name and in the City of London. See also **local government**.

meaningful the terms significant or full of meaning are preferable, and never use "meaningful dialogue".

means singular or plural as appropriate: "There is only one means to this end"; "His means are modest".

measures see **abbreviations**, **scientific measurements**.

media this word is plural; avoid it when you can.

medical terms never use medical nomenclature metaphorically, as in geriatric, paralytic, schizophrenic, spastic.

Bacteria and *viruses* are quite different and the two terms are not interchangeable. If there is any doubt about which caused an outbreak, use "micro-organism". Never use the American colloquialism "bug" for either. Antibiotics are used to treat bacterial but not viral infections.

Common terms The word inoculation has no double *n*; aneurysm (not aneurism); ampoule; Caesarean section. Electrocardiographs, etc, are machines, electrocardiograms are the tracings made by them. In words ending -*tomy* (eg, appendicectomy, hysterectomy, tonsillectomy), the word "operation" is tautologous. Many drugs are trade names and should be given uc, but try to use generic names wherever possible; check all drugs with *Extra pharmacopeia*. See also **drugs**, **trade names**.

Food poisoning The salmonellas often cause poisoning. When a particular species is referred to, it is printed in italics, eg, *Salmonella typhi* (see also **biological terms**). Note the spelling dysentery, not dysentry; dyspepsia.

X-rays The colloquialism "an X-ray" for an X-ray examination is common usage, as is the verb to X-ray. But avoid "The X-ray was sent to a specialist for diagnosis". X-rays are the form of radiation used to examine the patient or to take photographs, and the term should be restricted to this sense. Use "The X-ray photograph ...".

medieval is lc, and spelt thus (not -*iaeval*).

medium of communication, plural media (eg, mass media), but mediums (spiritualists). "Media coverage" is common usage, but try to be more specific.

megawatts the *capacity* of a power station is measured in megawatts. They indicate the rate at which it can produce electricity, just as top speed indicates the rate at which a car can travel.

The *output* of a power station is measured in megawatt hours. They indicate the total output over time, and are the product of the rate in megawatts multiplied by the time in hours for which that rate is maintained.

Do not confuse these terms.

members of Parliament takes lc *m*, but MP, no points. Plural MPs.

memorandum the plural is memorandums, not -*a*.

metropolitan lc except in titles. Although "in the Metropolis" sometimes refers to London, every big city is a metropolis and the usage should be avoided.

metropolitan magistrate not metropolitan police magistrate, see **courts**.

Michelangelo is spelt thus.

microchip is one word: chip is acceptable in context.

midday is one word.

Middle Ages takes uc.

Middle East the term encompasses the following: Bahrain, Cyprus, Egypt, Iran, Iraq, Israel, Jordan, Kuwait, Lebanon, Oman, Qatar, Saudi Arabia, Sudan, Syria, Turkey, United Arab Emirates, Yemen. In a general sense it also takes in the countries of the Maghreb: Algeria, Libya, Mauritania, Morocco, Tunisia, Western Sahara. Do not use Near East or the American term Mideast.

Middlesbrough has only one *o*.

MiG the former Soviet aircraft is spelt thus.

migrant not to be used for emigrant or immigrant. It refers to somebody who is in the process of migrating, rather than to one who has completed the process.

milage not mileage.

military nomenclature the word nowadays tends to refer to all services. Strictly an adjective, the phrase "the military" is common usage for all defence forces and interests. If you mean just soldiers, say army. See also **air force**, **naval nomenclature**.

Regiments and formations
Follow Army List. Note that infantry regiments and some armoured regiments are prefaced The (uc). Of the regiments in the Household Division only The Life Guards follows this practice. All titles take uc.

Companies: A Company, B Battery, 94 (Locating) Battery, C Squadron

Battalions: 1st, 2nd, etc, and 1st/5th, 61 Field Regiment, RA

Brigades: 24 Infantry Brigade, 5 Airborne Brigade

Divisions: 7th Armoured Division

Corps: X Corps, XII Corps

Armies: First Army

Army Groups: 21 Army Group

Ranks and abbreviations
General, Gen; Lieutenant General, Lt Gen; Major General, Maj Gen; Brigadier, Brig; Colonel, Col; Lieutenant Colonel, Lt Col; Major, Maj; Captain, Capt; Lieutenant, Lt; Second Lieutenant, 2nd Lt; Warrant Officer Class 1, WO1; Warrant Officer Class 2, WO2; Staff Sergeant, S Sgt; Sergeant, Sgt; Corporal, Cpl; Bombardier, Bdr; Lance Corporal, L Cpl; Private, Pte; Guardsman, Gdsmn; Gunner, Gnr; Rifleman, Rfn.

Beware other rank equivalents: Sapper, Spr; Driver, Dvr; Trooper, Tpr.

Appointments, ranks and titles
1 An appointment is a post held by an individual, not a rank. In *The Times* appointments count as job descriptions and take lc unless they are formal titles, thus: chief of the general staff, adjutant general, judge advocate, general officer commanding, commanding officer, officer commanding, regimental sergeant major,

company quartermaster sergeant, non-commissioned officer (NCO).

2 Chief of the defence staff (CDS). A navy chief of the defence staff becomes Admiral Sir John Jones; an army one is Field Marshal Sir John Jones; and an RAF one Marshal of the Royal Air Force Sir John Jones, in each case followed by, Chief of the Defence Staff.

3 Do not abbreviate field marshal to FM. A field marshal would be either a peer or a knight, so the correct follow-up for Field Marshal Sir Richard Vincent, for example, should be Sir Richard.

4 An officer with a personal title should be described in full on the first occasion. Thus: Lieutenant General (or Lt Gen) Sir John Jones, subsequently Sir John or General Jones.

5 All regimental sergeant majors (RSMs) are WO1s (see **6** below) but not all WO1s are RSMs. There are also a few senior WO1s in the Royal Army Ordnance Corps with the rank of conductor "WO1 (conductor) ...".

6 The rank of warrant officer belongs to the RAF; it is not an army rank. Soldiers are always either warrant officer 1 (the senior of the two) or warrant officer 2.

7 Remember the rule, to capitalise titles not jobs. Thus Corporal Jones (or Cpl in lists), but the corporal, the general, the sergeant. Do not use Mr when writing about soldiers. Use abbreviated form of the rank unless writing "the general" or "the captain".

Common terms

battalions: a number of infantry regiments have more than one battalion now, so check with Army List.

beating retreat, not beating the retreat.

guards of honour are ceremonial troops used to meet visiting dignitaries. Like all guards they are mounted, as sentries are posted.

infantry, artillery, etc (army or service), lc.

The King's Own Royal Border Regiment (full official form).

King's Troop, RHA remains King's Troop even when the monarch is a queen.

Last Post (not the) is sounded (not played).

parade: troops do not parade through the streets, they march.

Royal Corps of Signals, contract to Royal Signals or R Signals (not RCS).

Royal Engineers: RE (never REs).

Royal Welch Fusiliers, not Royal Welsh Fusiliers.

A sergeant major in the Household Cavalry (The Life Guards and the Blues and Royals) is known as a corporal major, and a sergeant as a corporal of horse. There are also corporals in the Household Cavalry. In the foot guards a lance corporal is known as a corporal and a corporal is known as a lance sergeant.

Special Air Service: regiment, SAS. (For SBS, see **naval nomenclature**.)

Trooping the Colour (not Trooping *of* the Colour). Colours are carried by infantry regiments; the cavalry equivalent is a guidon, the artillery equivalent is a gun.

trumpeters, buglers: cavalry regiments have trumpeters, the infantry buglers. They are not interchangeable terms.

militate (against or in favour of) does not mean mitigate.

millennia plural of millennium. Remember that not all Latin plurals are common usage, eg, forums, memorandums.

milliard of French origin and means a thousand million, but use billion.

millions write out millions from one million to nine million, thereafter use numerals: 10 million, etc.

Abbreviate only for currencies and headlines, eg, £15m. Decimal notation (£17.2m) is to be used only of currency and to only two decimal places, except in tables and passages with a high frequency of numerals. Write, two and a half million, or 19 million.

minimal is a superlative of little. Do not use minor or minimal to mean small or very small, only smaller or smallest.

minister as in minister of health, etc, lc.

ministry lc except in formal title (Ministry of Defence). Check if a department is or is not a ministry. Avoid MoD except in headlines, use defence ministry.

minus opposite of plus in arithmetical sentences. Otherwise, the word *without* or a negative construction is preferable.

minuscule (not miniscule) is not a variant of small. It should be confined to the medieval script or to a strictly appropriate metaphor. Use tiny.

misfire is one word.

Miss see **Ms, appellations**.

mistress see **girl friend**.

mitigate does not mean militate, however often you try to make it.

Mogul (not Mughal) for the empire and related works of art.

Mohammed see **Muhammad**.

monarch, the (lc), but the Sovereign and the Crown, when referring to the British monarch.

moneys not monies, but the singular will usually suffice; also moneyed not monied.

Mongol(ian) for the race takes uc. Those with Down's syndrome used to be mongols (lc) but no more.

moon, the is lc, except in an astronomical context to distinguish it from other moons. See also **space, sun**.

Mori not MORI. This is now a voiced abbreviation in common usage, as with Ciba, Esso, Rospa, etc. See also **initials**.

Moslem use Muslim. See also **Islam**.

mosquitoes plural, not -*os*.

motorcade is now common usage.

motor cycle is two words.

MP plural MPs, members of Parliament (in the UK), of the parliament (lc) elsewhere.

Mr, Mrs, Miss, Ms no points.

Ms use for married or unmarried women where requested in Britain, and unless requested otherwise in stories from America. See also **appellations**.

Mughal see **Mogul**.

Muhammad the approved *Times* spelling of the Prophet's name, but respect other spellings of similar first names commonly used throughout the Middle

East. Do not use Muhammadan or Muhammadanism, use Muslim. See also **Arabic names**, **Islam**.

Mujahid plural Mujahidin, fighter(s) in a jihad, or holy war.

musical nomenclature try to avoid abbreviations. But piano is accepted for pianoforte and cello (no apostrophe) for violoncello. Proms is permitted. Use pianissimo and fortissimo (not *pp* and *ff*). Phantasy is a form distinct from fantasy and fantasia. Accept a performer's spelling of his own name as given on his own programme. Note these spellings: Chaliapin, Diaghilev, Stravinsky, Tchaikovsky.

TITLES OF WORKS

1 Italics are used for the following: titles of operas, oratorios, cantatas, ballets (Wagner's *Die Meistersinger*, Brahms's *Song of Destiny*, Rimsky-Korsakov's *Scheherazade*), official names of symphonies and symphonic poems (Berlioz's *Symphonie fantastique*, Strauss's *Don Juan*, Sibelius's *Tapiola*), names of smaller instrumental works (Elgar's *Pomp and Circumstance* marches, Schumann's *Carnaval*).

2 Quotation marks and initial capitals are used for titles of smaller vocal pieces, songs, part songs, madrigals, anthems, motets, names of tunes, and parts of the church service of whatever language (Brahms's "Die Mainacht", Stanford's "The Blue Bird"), titles or first words of arias or movements in operas, oratorios, or large church works ("Voi che Sapete" from *Figaro*, the "Agnus Dei" in Beethoven's Missa Solemnis, "Vouchsafe, O Lord" in Handel's Dettingen Te Deum).

3 Initial capitals are given to instrumental works commonly known by keys or opus numbers (Beethoven's Eroica Symphony, Beethoven's Sonata, opus III, Beethoven's Mass in C), and for generic works (Verdi's Requiem, Beethoven's Missa Solemnis).

Note that names of musical forms (sonata, symphony, suite, etc) do not take uc apart from their use as titles, so: "The last period of Beethoven's sonatas begins with the Sonata in A, opus 101". Compositions known by their number are given thus: Chopin's fourth ballade, Beethoven's seventh symphony. (But Beethoven's Ninth is common usage.)

TECHNICAL TERMS

Terms of foreign origin now accepted into the English language are written without italics, quotes or capitals. French terms of this kind drop their accents. Italian terms generally, but not always, take English plurals: allegro, andante, aria, cello, coda, continuo, crescendo(s), decrescendo, diminuendo, ensemble, finale, forte (fortissimo), largo, leitmotif (plural leitmotifs), lento, lieder (singular song), obbligato, opus (plural works), piano (pianissimo), prima donna(s), rallentando, scherzo, tempo (plural tempi), timpani, trio(s).

Names of instruments or organ stops of foreign origin (cor anglais, vox humana) should be treated in the same way.

There are necessary exceptions. Terms liable to be confused with English usage must be quoted, eg, "grave". Terms less generally accepted in English, notably those of the ballet, must be in italics, eg, *entrechat, pointes*. Phrases, whether actually taken from the score or not, must be in italics, eg, "The *sul ponticello* bowing of the *più tranquillo* passage in the *allegro giocoso ma non troppo*" (if you must). Such terms as Finale, Trio take uc where used of specific pieces: "The Trio in the Scherzo of Beethoven's Ninth", but "The solo for viola d'amore is in the nature of a trio since it is followed by a complete reprise".

music-hall is hyphenated.

Muslim not Moslem, Mohamedan, Muselman. See

also **Islam**, **Muhammad**.

mute *e* if there is to be any consistency in keeping or dropping the final mute *e* in words taking the suffixes *-able*, *-age*, *-ing*, *-ish*, a rule is needed. Fowler has one that is simple and sensible: drop the *e* unless it is needed to emphasise the soft sound of a preceding *c* or *g*. Thus changeable, knowledgeable, singeing (from singe — soft *g* must be emphasised to distinguish from singing), swingeing, traceable. Observance of the rule leads to a few unusual but defensible forms: aging, debatable, milage, ratable. When in doubt consult a standard dictionary: in all cases where an alternative spelling without the *e* is given, that is the one to be used in *The Times*. Remember, the English language should be allowed to evolve, under pressure of common usage, in the direction of simplicity.

N

naive, naivety not naif, naïveté, no dieresis.

names people are entitled to be known as they want to be known, provided that their identities are clear. When somebody elects to change his or her name, as when Cassius Clay became Muhammad Ali, give both names until the new name is widely known. See also **appellations**, **doctor**.

national avoid as synonym for citizen, as in "a French national".

national anthem is lc.

National Health Service NHS after first mention.

nationalise like privatise, this can cover many different forms of ownership. Try to specify the size and form of public ownership, for instance majority shareholding, etc. See also **quango**.

nationalist lc except when referring to the official name of a political party.

National Theatre now the Royal National Theatre.

National Trust this is a charity. Gifts to the NT should not be described as gifts to the nation.

Nato not NATO.

naval nomenclature when referring to the navy, use Royal Navy, US Navy, etc. Refer to a naval ship as HMS *Achilles* or the *Achilles*. Submarines are boats, not ships; marines are lc but Royal Marines uc. The fleet is lc now that there is just one.

Ranks and abbreviations
Admiral, Adm; Commodore, Cdre; Captain, Capt; Commander, Cdr; Lieutenant Commander, Lt Cdr; Lieutenant, Lt; Chief Petty Officer, CPO; Leading Seaman, L/S.

Ranks and commands
1 Remember that job descriptions are lc, titles used before names or where a formal title might be confused with a job take uc. The captain of a ship is the officer appointed to command it and is referred to as the commanding officer. His rank is not necessarily Captain, Royal Navy. For example: a frigate could be commanded by a Captain, RN, or a Commander, both of whom are captains of their ship but are titled by their rank. Royal Navy shore establishments, eg, HMS *Daedalus*, also have captains.

2 Royal Navy (or RN) should be added after rank and

name for all officers below rank of Commodore.

3 A flag officer is a rear admiral or above, exercising command and authorised by the Admiralty to fly a flag. Flag lieutenants, flag captains are staff officers to flag officers, not officers of flag rank.

4 Admirals' appointments should not be confused with their rank. The following are flag ranks: Admiral of the Fleet, admiral, vice admiral, rear admiral. Guidance on appointments and capitals: "Admiral Sir John Smith, GCB, ADC to be Chief of Naval Staff and First Sea Lord"; "Rear Admiral James Jones, CB, to be Flag Officer Flotilla 1". The rank Admiral of the Fleet is the highest naval rank. It is a formal title and takes uc but does not refer to a job or command of any fleet. For example, the Duke of Edinburgh is an Admiral of the Fleet, whereas the fleet is actually commanded by an admiral whose job title is Commander in Chief Fleet (CinC Fleet).

5 Follow correct style for hyphenation. Hyphens are not used for Commandant General, Royal Marines; Surgeon Captain, Instructor Commander, Lieutenant Commander.

6 Ratings, not "other ranks" in the navy (but "other ranks" in the marines). And remember signalman, not signaller.

Ships

liner normally refers to a large passenger ship that plies a regular route. There are few nowadays.

ships should generally be treated as feminine (though taking that/which not who), but *it* is more appropriate in technical passages, specification, etc. Ships are not christened; they are named.

ships' names should be preceded by HMS or *the*: "the *QE2*".

shipowner: a person or company owning or managing ships. The owner objects to being called a shipper, who is a person who ships or arranges for the shipment of goods.

s.s., m.v., etc, should not normally be used. More relevant information for general news is contained in the phrases "the liner *QE2*", "the tanker *Vexilla*", "the cargo ship *Rita*".

tonnage: for passenger ships give gross tonnage (internal cubic capacity). For cargo ships give deadweight tonnage (carrying capacity). Thus the tanker *Vexilla*, 32,000 tons deadweight, can carry 32,000 tons of oil and bunkers. Agency copy should be checked with Lloyd's Register, which lists gross and deadweight tonnage of all merchant ships. It is not necessary to specify in copy which type of tonnage is given except where confusion is possible.

Common terms

alter (not change) course.

astern (never behind or following): eg, the *Achilles* was astern of the *Ajax*.

the *Britannia* (royal yacht) is HMY, not HMS.

embarked in: not on.

line ahead: not astern.

moored or made fast: vessels are never tied up.

on board: do not say aboard.

pennant: not pendant.

RN (ret): use for retired officers below rank of commodore.

SBS: now called Special Boat Service (not Special Boat Squadron).

tow: the towing ship has the towed ship *in* tow; the towed ship is *under* tow.

Union Flag: not Union Jack in naval contexts, except when flown at the jackstaff.

under way, not weigh anchor.

Nazi uc for the German party, nazi (lc) as a term of abuse. See also **fascist**.

Negro see **blacks**.

net not nett. Net Book Agreement takes uc to avoid confusion with any deal on fishing manuals.

Netherlands, The the proper name of the country, but Holland is shorter and means the same.

Newcastle upon Tyne no hyphens.

New College, Oxford do not omit the word College or the comma after it. Do not omit Oxford unless the context is clear.

New Haven (Connecticut), Newhaven (Sussex).

newscaster prefer newsreader.

News International Rupert Murdoch is chairman and chief executive of the News Corporation, an international company that can be described in second mentions as News Corp. A subsidiary of News Corp is News International, a British company that owns Times Newspapers Holdings. It owns *The Times*, *The Sunday Times* and the three Times Supplements. Andrew Knight is executive chairman of News International and thus, for practical purposes, of *The Times*. Mr Murdoch does not "own" any of these companies, though his family is the dominant and controlling, though *not* majority, shareholder in News Corp. See also *The Times*.

newspapers, journals use italics for titles (see also **italics**). Cap and italicise the *The* if it is part of the masthead, but not when the journal's name is used merely adjectivally: "the *Times* reporter wrote ...". Cap *L* in the definite article in titles of French newspapers, eg, *Le Figaro*, *Le Monde*. In Scandinavian titles the suffix *-et* or *-en* is equivalent to "the", eg, *Aftenposten*, *Svenska Dagbladet*, etc, so do not say "the *Aftenposten*". Note also: *Izvestia, Neue Zürcher Zeitung, New York Herald Tribune* (no hyphen), *The New York Times, Times of India, The Washington Post, Die Welt.*

When quoting material from another newspaper in *The Times*, always give the reference. Do not use "reports in another newspaper". But the phrase "media reports" may be used when material has been generally disseminated.

new year but New Year's day.

no the old *Times* style book speaks true: "One of the most useful words in the English language". Use this splendid word as often as possible and you will shorten many a sentence: not "There was a total absence of wind" but "There was no wind". Similarly, not "The reaction of the audience was negative" but "The audience did not like it", etc.

non- the prefix is a convenient device for negative words that have no exact opposite and for designating a class from which a named subclass is excluded, eg, non-European, non-ferrous metals. But restraint is needed. Avoid *non-* formations when there is another negative form (non-accessible for inaccessible), or when there is an appropriate opposite (non-sick for well or healthy). Avoid other cumbersome compounds such as non-working class, non-card-carrying communists. See also **hyphens**.

nonconformist (lc) but the Nonconformist Church and Nonconformist churches (buildings). See also **church**.

none is short for not one and is singular. However, on rare occasions a plural construction is permissible: "None of them are better singers than the Welsh", and to avoid the him/her inelegance: "None of them have done their best ...". See also **bisexual pronouns**.

nonetheless one word.

noon not 12 noon.

no one preferably use *nobody* except in emphatic constructions such as "no one person knew ...".

normalcy should be left to the Americans, who popularised it; the English word is normality.

north see **compass points**.

northeast, northwest, northeasterly one word. See also **compass points**.

Northern Ireland generally preferable term to "Ulster". No term referring to the parties and factions is uncontroversial, nor is the name. Avoid references to religion if possible, ie, republican rather than Catholic, unionist rather than Protestant (both lc except in titles of organisations). Avoid the word terrorist except in reference to appropriate incidents, prefer the use of paramilitary of the IRA, UDA, etc. Avoid Loyalist if possible, but always use cap L. Never contrast "terrorist IRA" with "Loyalist paramilitaries". Never let comment creep into news by the back door of terminology. See also **Ireland, Irish Republican Army, Loyalist, terrorism**.

Northumberland is a county. **Northumbria** is a health, police and tourist authority.

not only requires a *but* and, almost always, an *also* or a *moreover*, etc. "London buses are not only red but often green as well" is acceptable.

noun-compounds though ugly, are part of a living language. Hence, sit-in, stand-off, kick-off, shake-out, walk-out. New ones might be put in a quarantine of inverted commas for a while.

nouns as adjectives the practice of stringing nouns together without prepositions ought to be checked. Phrases like "world oil supply situation", "drug traffic increase", "aircraft crash victims inquest" are to be avoided. There is more excuse for the practice in headlines, but headlines in this form can be ambiguous: "Miners dispute deal".

nuclear terms should be used with precision.

Fission and fusion Fission means a nuclear reaction in which the nucleus of a heavy atom splits into two roughly equal fragments and a number of neutrons. Fusion means a reaction in which two light nuclei combine to form a heavier one, usually emitting a neutron. Fission operates in nuclear reactors and A-bombs; fusion in H-bombs and thermonuclear or fusion reactions.

Fissile and fertile Fissile (not fissionable) materials (uranium 234, uranium 233, plutonium) are those in which a chain fission reaction can be maintained (ie, they are usable in A-bombs or reactors). Fertile materials (uranium 238, thorium) are those that can be converted into fissile material in a nuclear reactor. A reactor is said to breed if it produces more fissile material than it consumes.

Nuclear and thermonuclear The term nuclear applies to any reaction or device involving nuclear reactions: it therefore includes thermonuclear, which denotes reactions brought about by high temperatures (in practice, fusion reactions). Do not use these terms as metaphors.

Kiloton and megaton A kiloton weapon is one with a release of energy equal to that of a thousand tons of

TNT; a megaton weapon equals a million tons of TNT. A weapon described as "in the megaton range" must be thermonuclear; but smaller thermonuclear weapons can be made.

numbers write from one to ten in full, 11 upwards in numerals, unless they are an approximation, eg, "about twenty people turned up". A hundred, not one hundred, when written in full. One in five is singular, two in five are plural. In a numerical sequence, if any number is written in letters (ie, is below 11), then all must be: "The number of injured rose from nine to twelve". But it is permitted to use numerals below 11 in sequences for the sake of clarity: "Inflation has risen from 2 per cent to 6 per cent to 12 per cent". All numbers at the start of a sentence must be written in full, which means avoiding huge ones in this position. With large numbers, apply the rule of three (ie, that only three numbers can be comprehended): profits of £12,310,678 should be £12.3m, of £123,106 should be £123,000, £12,310 should be £12,300 etc. This applies especially in headlines. Million and billion should be written out and kept singular. When referring to money, the terms may be abbreviated: £15m, £2bn. The number 0.5 and above is rounded up, below 0.5 is rounded down.

Ordinals Write out up to hundredth, then 101st, 122nd, etc. But names are different:

42nd Street, 38th parallel, etc.

Fractions Compounds such as half-hour, half-day, half-dozen, etc, take a hyphen. Half an hour, half a day, half a dozen do not. Fractions take hyphens when used as adjectives but not as nouns, eg, two-thirds full, but two thirds of the people questioned. Generally speaking one third, one half and so on mean an exact proportion; a third, a half, are approximations. Numbers between one and two containing a fraction are singular. It is better to write a mile and a half instead of one and a half miles; two and a half miles is correct. In stories

involving statistics or precise figures, decimals are
nowadays preferable and easier on the eye.

O

obituaries these must follow house style. There is
separate style guidance for the formal obituaries.
References to the deceased in any form should avoid
vacuous adjectives and tendentious superlatives such as
"greatest ever" or, worse, "possibly greatest ever".

oblivious of means forgetful of and unaware of, not
ignorant or uncomprehending.

obscenities (and profanities, vulgarities) some writers
regard these as a sign of literary virility. As in spoken
English, they are a sign of weakness, an inability to
make a strong point other than by causing verbal
offence. "Four-letter words" upset most readers and
should be avoided. In direct quotes, where they are
essential to the story, soften them with dots "f...", "c...".
In an article specifically about obscenity, where readers
might be considered adequately warned, this rule might
be relaxed, but this should be a decision for the editor,
the ultimate arbiter of taste (and style) in *The Times*.

octopuses are spelt thus, not octopi.

of avoid the use of an adjective plus *of* as a genteel
substitute for a strong verb, as in "caring of" for care or
"indicative of" for indicate.

of all time as in "best footballer of all time", is banned.
It is certainly untrue.

old age pensioners or pensioners (not OAPs), now

officially known as senior citizens. Beware further changes in taste.

Old Masters capitalised to avoid confusion. Do not hyphenate where used adjectivally: Old Master paintings.

O level noun (no hyphen) but O-level as adjective. Distinguish from GCSEs, etc.

ombudsman, -woman now common usage.

on account of the fact the words because or since are preferable.

one be careful about this word when using it as a first person singular. Try to avoid references to the writer in copy. Such words as *one*, *us* and *you* tend to read as affectation. If a critic or columnist must refer to him/herself, be honest and use *I* and *me*. Above all, avoid a mix of these pronouns in one piece. That said, *one* is better than *you*. In a different sense, *one* is too often used after an adjective where it is not necessary. For "The game was a keenly contested one" write "The game was keenly contested".

only take care to place this word according to meaning. She *only* touched the key but did not press it; she touched *only* the key, not the switch; she touched the *only* key. Only should go immediately before the word it qualifies.

on to two words should always be preferred to one, but "They stepped onto the boat" is acceptable.

opencast one word.

operation a sloppy word, like situation, best avoided

except in reference to medicine and war.

ophthalmic not opthalmic.

optimal, optimum are often no more than showy substitutes for best or ideal or most favourable. Optimum implies the best adjustment for a particular end of several conflicting factors. If there are no conflicting factors, use a simpler word.

or need not be preceded by *either*, though it is strengthened thereby if only two options are mentioned. Avoid a comma before it unless for the sake of clarification. See also **punctuation**.

oral see **verbal**.

order paper is lc.

Orders in Council are approved, not signed, by the Queen.

ordinary shares and preference shares, lc.

Organisation of Petroleum Exporting Countries known as Opec.

orient (verb), prefer orientate; the Orient (noun), prefer East. See also **compass points**.

Orkney or the Orkney Islands, not the Orkneys.

or otherwise the use of this expression in such phrases as "the accuracy or otherwise" is generally superfluous.

outdoor one word as adjective; the noun is outdoors.

over in some contexts "more than" is better ("I walked

more than fifty miles; I ate more than a dozen eggs")
but there can be no precise rule on the point.

overall one word as adjective, but use sparingly.

overwhelming often means big or large, both much
better words.

Oxford and Cambridge avoid lumping them together
in a story about education. There are other universities
in Britain. Avoid the term Oxbridge except in quotes.

P

Pakistani for natives of Pakistan or of Pakistan origin.
Be careful of its application to British immigrant
communities, which may be Bangladeshi, Bengali,
Indian, Punjabi, etc. Do not use Pakistani as an
adjective for Pakistan. Say the Pakistan army or
Pakistan culture.

palace lc except when part of a name, eg Blenheim
Palace; "the Palace" is an acceptable short form for
Buckingham Palace in stories about the royal family.

palaeo- not *paleo-*, so palaeography, etc.

paragraphing a paragraph, says Gowers, is "a unit of
thought, not of length ... homogeneous in subject
matter and sequential in treatment of it". See also
Introduction.

paralyse may be used in a metaphorical sense, but
paralytic never, least of all as a term of abuse. See also
medical terms.

paratroops a general term for troops dropped by parachute. A parachutist is a specialist in the activity.

Pardo Palace a royal palace on the outskirts of Madrid; the Prado is the Madrid art gallery.

parentheses correct word for round brackets. Like capitals and dashes, they look ugly in a column of type and should be avoided whenever possible. Prefer the humble comma or rebuild the sentence. See also **brackets**, **punctuation**.

parliamentary documents are lettered HC (for Commons) and HL (for Lords) and numbering starts again each session. It is necessary to say "HC12 (1991–2)" and so on. See also **government papers**.

parliamentary nomenclature See also **capitalisation**.

Act: uc only in reference to a formal statute: Finance Act, but the local finance acts.

adjournment: means conclusion of debate, as in: "The House adjourned at ...".

applause: never, always "cheers" or "hear, hear".

backbench (adj), backbencher: one word.

beginning of debate: The Lord Chancellor took his seat on the Woolsack at 2.30 pm. The Speaker took the Chair at 2.30 pm.

bill: lc until passed, when it becomes an act, also lc except in the formal title. A bill in the Commons is presented, read *a* first time, read *a* second time, read *the* third time. In the Lords it is introduced and read *a* first time, read *a* second time, read *the* third time, and passed. Bills are considered *in* committee, and are considered *on* report.

Chair, the: takes uc.

chamber, the: takes lc.

closure: as in "move the closure".

committee: departmental, joint select, standing, etc,

are all lc to avoid alphabet soup, including public accounts committee. Only use capitals when "the House is in Committee" or in a title, as "Chairman of Committees".

committee stage: of a bill, comes between second and third reading.

constituency names: spelling to follow that in *The Times Guide to the House of Commons*. East, West, Central, etc, to be spelt out.

deputy speakers: there are two deputy speakers. They should be set up thus: the Deputy Speaker, Mr John Jones.

early day motion: all lc.

election, by-election, general election: all lc.

front bench: two words, lc; frontbencher, one word.

galleries: lc, but the Press Gallery, Strangers' Gallery.

guillotine: no quotation marks.

House of Lords officers: the Clerk of the Parliaments, the Clerk Assistant (of the Parliaments), the Reading Clerk (of the House of Lords), no hyphens.

Leader of the House: takes uc, but everybody else is a leader, lc, including the leader of the Opposition.

Lower House: takes uc.

member of Parliament: capitalised thus; MP, no points.

Opposition Chief Whip: takes uc.

order, order paper: take lc.

parliamentary private secretary: is lc, but PPS (no points).

part I, part II, etc, of a bill.

party labels: follow those used in *The Times Guide to the House of Commons*.

private member's bill: all lc.

question, question time, prime minister's questions.

Serjeant at Arms: (no hyphens), note spelling. See also **sergeant**.

Speaker, the: takes uc.

Supply day: uc to avoid confusion.

table of the House: uc only when personified, eg, "the Table refused this question".

three-line whip: lc, hyphenated thus.

Treasury bench: capitalised thus.

Upper House: takes uc.

Vote (of money): takes uc.

whips (party): are lc, but Chief Whip.

parliaments is lc, as are parliamentary, parliamentary Labour party, etc, but Houses of Parliament and Parliament (with no "the") in references to the British parliament, as in "she entered Parliament in 1965".

partially, partly partially is of degree, partly of extension: partially deaf, partly under the water. Avoid partially as simply a genteel synonym of partly.

party lc except where integral to an official name in common usage, eg, Social Democratic and Labour Party (SDLP). But Labour, Conservative and Communist parties, lc. See also **capitalisation**.

past use past rather than last in such phrases as "the past two weeks". See also **last**.

past tense of verbs always prefer the shorter form using terminal -*t* where appropriate, eg, spelt not spelled, learnt not learned.

Paymaster General takes uc, no hyphen.

peacock strictly applies only to the male; the female is a peahen. Both are peafowl, but peacock is common usage for the species.

pedlar avoid the American spelling, peddler. Somebody who pedals a bicycle is a pedaller.

peers a peer or peeress has a seat in the House of Lords. A female life peer is a peeress referred to normally as Baroness Smith. Not all lords or ladies are peers — some are the offspring of earls, etc, or wives of knights — although "the peerage" is common usage for the nobility as a whole, which does not include baronets and knights. After the first mention of the Marquess of Paddington, Earl of Euston, Viscount Pimlico or Lord Holborn, call them all Lord Paddington, Euston, etc. That is how they sign themselves. Usually just say, the peer or peeress (if in the House of Lords). See also **titles**.

pence the abbreviation for pence is p (no point).

people always preferable to persons, except where the identity of each person in a group needs emphasis or in expressions such as "the law is no respecter of persons".

per *a* is preferable with an English noun (a year, a mile) provided its use does not lead to ambiguity. Thus, "six miles an hour" but "production per man hour".

per cent two words, no full point. Do not use % except in a heavily statistical article for the sake of brevity or in graphics and headlines.

percentage, proportion cut down on these words. When they mean no more than part, use part. For "a proportion of the profits was retained", write "part of the profits ...". Similarly, for "a large percentage of parents" write "many parents". Beware of percentages in economic, political and statistical stories. If the mortgage rate goes up from 10 per cent to 11 per cent it has not risen by one per cent. It has risen by ten per cent or one percentage point. A political party whose support has fallen from 50 per cent to 40 per cent has lost 20 per cent or ten percentage points.

perestroika not italic.

Persia write Iran for the modern state. For Persian Gulf, see also **Gulf**.

person see **people**.

personnel use people or employees whenever possible.

phalangist in Lebanon, but falangist in Spain.

phenomenon plural, phenomena. Phenomenal has a technical meaning in philosophy and is a cliché when used as a synonym of remarkable or big.

-phile bibliophile, anglophile, not *-phil*.

Philhellenic takes uc.

phone no apostrophe; permissible abbreviation in headlines only.

piecework is one word.

pilgrims are lc, but Pilgrim Fathers for those who sailed from Plymouth in 1620.

place-names use *The Times Atlas of the World*. Anglicise when an English name is in common usage (use *Webster's New Geographical Dictionary*). Hence Rome, Venice, Brussels, Florence, Prague, Geneva, Moscow, Naples, The Hague, Mexico City, Peking (see also **Chinese names**).

Plaid Cymru (Welsh Nationalist party): never shorten to "the Plaid".

plc lc no points, but can usually be dropped.

plurals always try to avoid the plural where the singular will do. Singulars are more specific and carry more force: "A man's got to do what a man's got to do ..." rather than "Men have got to do ...". Hence always make corporate bodies and institutions singular unless this looks odd: "The National Trust is ...". Sports teams are usually plural: "Arsenal/England are struggling." See also **collective nouns**.

plus, minus do not use as variants of "and/without", as in "He had five courses plus coffee, and then left minus his hat". They belong to arithmetic.

poetess use poet; see also **feminine designations**.

Poet Laureate is always uc; the plural is Poets Laureate.

police courts use magistrates' courts; see also **courts**.

police ranks avoid hyphens whenever possible. Use lc except in official titles and before names. Abbreviate detective and superintendent when preceding a name to Det and Supt. A (woman) police constable and detective constable (Det Con before names) should be (W)PC and constable after first mention. PC is permissible in headlines. Police sergeant and detective sergeant both become sergeant after the first mention. Inspector and all ranks above are referred to as Mr after the first mention. When referring to a chief constable or equivalent avoid the phrase police chief except in headlines. Use uc for an established institution, eg, Serious Fraud office, but when there are many use lc, eg, special branch (presumably Metropolitan or local).

"political correctness" the English language, especially in the USA, has become infected by a new authoritarianism, designed to use changes in style to make political statements, often on the pretext that style does that already. The usual method is by overblown euphemisms and clumsy circumlocutions. That said, every newspaper needs to be careful of all normative or emotional phrases, especially those referring to women and race. A story should not cause needless offence. But resist absurd neologisms that obscure meaning and patronise their subjects, such as "physically challenged" for disabled. See also **feminine designations**, **race**.

poll tax acceptable word for the former community charge, now council tax.

Pope the present one is capitalised, but popes, lc.

position like situation, an empty, overworked word, as in "the employment position is unchanged". Try to rephrase such sentences. For "in a position to", "able to" or "can" are preferable.

possibly like most qualifiers, possibly can often be omitted with benefit.

post codes should not be used except when giving an address for information. In news stories always give a city's name after a particular district unless the district is well known. Use "in Bayswater, London", not "in London's Bayswater"; "Moss Side, Manchester", not "Manchester's Moss Side".

Post Office for the corporation; post office (lc) for the branches; sub-post office, sub-postmaster.

postwar, prewar never to be used as adverbs as in "There were a million unemployed prewar". Write before/after the war. The normal reference to war in such phrases is still to the second world war, but beware of the context.

pound do not use the sign £ by itself, except in headings.

power stations kilowatt and megawatt are units of the rate of generation or consumption of electrical energy, whereas kilowatt-hour and megawatt-hour are measures of quantity. Kilowatt-hour is the unit of electricity bills. Hence kilowatts (megawatts) are correct for the generating capacity of a station: kilowatt-hours (megawatt-hours) for output during a stated period, usually a year. See also **megawatts**.

practical, practicable beware. "Safety lies in remembering that *practicable* means capable of being effected or accomplished, and that *practical* means adapted to actual conditions" (Fowler). The negative forms are unpractical and impracticable.

practically has two uses: almost, and in a practical way. Try to avoid it in the former sense, thereby rendering it more vigorous in the latter.

practice is a noun; practise is a verb.

praesidium not presidium.

predecessor means person who predeceases another. But the word has entered common usage in its metaphorical sense: "Mr Major's predecessor, Mrs Thatcher". The more correct word, forerunner, tends to imply a closer association than predecessor.

prefer(red) but proffer(ed).

premier do not use premier for prime minister. Premier may be used of the heads of government of Canadian provinces and Australian states. Resist the word premiership. Use prime-ministership.

premiere may nowadays be used as both a noun and a verb, for an artistic debut or to give one.

premise an assumption in an argument. Premises, a piece of property, are plural. Do not use premiss(es).

prepositional verbs these proliferate: check up on, consult with, face up to, measure up to, meet up with. Sometimes they are neat and useful formations (get on with, go back on, take up with). Sometimes they convey a nuance not present in the plain verb (compare check and check up on). Sometimes they are unnecessary variants for simple verbs (measure up to for reach or fit). Sometimes the preposition adds nothing of significance (consult with, meet with, stop off). Use with caution.

Pre-Raphaelite is capitalised thus.

Presbyterian beware especially with the adjective Scots. See also **church**.

present better than *current* but better still, reconstruct sentence using the word *now*. Presently tends to mean *soon*, not *now*, but this use varies, so *soon* is better.

president lc except in front of name. See also **capitalisation**.

press, the is lc.

preventive not preventative, an adjective.

prime minister unlike the various chancellors, there is only one prime minister in Britain and no reason to depart from the general rule that descriptive job titles are lc. Whereas President Bush is the American president, the prime minister is never Prime Minister Major. Except in quotes, "Mr Prime Minister..." always lc. The abbreviation, PM, is permitted in headlines. See also **capitalisation**, **premier**.

prince, princess see **titles**.

Princess of Wales and "the princess" after first mention (never Princess Diana).

Princes Street Edinburgh is spelt thus.

principal is an adjective and noun meaning capital, chief, head, important, main.

principle is a noun meaning concept, ideal, rule, underlying moral.

Privy Council takes uc, but privy counsellor (not councillor), lc.

probe only in a scientific or medical context. Police do not probe things, they look at, enquire into or investigate them.

problem every subject is becoming a "problem" that has to be "solved". The habit is both boring and misleading, since many so-called problems are really conflicts of interest, or forces to which nothing as final as a solution can be found. The word is cruelly overworked, like question and issue. Struggle to avoid using it.

Procurator Fiscal the Crown prosecutor in Scotland.

profanities see **obscenities**.

proportion see **percentage**.

pros and cons are spelt thus.

protagonist the original meaning is the leading actor in a (Greek) drama. A legitimate extension is a prominent supporter (of either side) in a debate or quarrel. It does not mean advocate or proponent.

Protestant takes uc; beware of using the term of all Christians who are not Roman Catholic. See also **church**, **Northern Ireland**.

prove has *proved* as a past participle in English: the word proven should be restricted to the Scottish verdict "not proven".

public house pub for short.

Public Record Office takes uc; not Records.

public school public-school boys/girls. But the term independent school is preferable. See also **education institutions**.

punctuation is made for man, not man for punctuation. It is a courtesy designed to help readers to understand a story without stumbling, not a fireworks display to show off your dashes and gaspers. Remember the first rule, the best punctuation is the full stop. Commas are best used to clarify lists and phrases within sentences, not to join them to other sentences. All other punctuation is second best.

Commas Do not enclose adverbs and adverbial phrases in commas unless they are unwieldy or need special emphasis. Too many commas obscure the main outline of a sentence: "He had not, previously, met the plaintiff, except when, in 1922, he had, unexpectedly, found himself in Paris." None of those commas is strictly necessary. The prime minister John Major (no comma) is acceptable though Joe Bloggs, a little-known singer, needs two. Omit the comma before *if, unless, before*, *since*, *when*, unless the rhythm or sense of the sentence demands it. Commas are not usually needed before or after *therefore* and *accordingly* but are needed before and after most uses of *however*, which is why that word should be used only for a substantial change of direction.

Words in apposition take a comma after as well as before: "Magdalen College, Oxford, is ..."; "On July 7, 1958, the ...". Avoid the so-called Oxford comma: *x, y and z* instead of *x, y, and z*.

Dashes Do not use for commas. Dashes are sloppy punctuation, ugly in narrow columns of newspaper type. They often indicate that a sentence is badly constructed and needs rewriting.

Semicolons are falling into disuse. They can be effective in breaking up a sequence of phrases where a comma is confusing. A full stop is generally preferable.

Colons are most commonly used to introduce lists. They throw attention forward to point a contrast or a parallel, but should be avoided otherwise. When listed items are on a separate line, use a colon followed by a dash.

Interrogation marks are used only with direct, never with indirect questions. They are not used with rhetorical questions.

Quotation marks Use double quotation marks, single for quotes inside double ones. Punctuation marks go inside the inverted commas if they relate to the words quoted, outside if they relate to the main sentence. If the whole sentence is a quotation the final point goes inside. So I said: "Why has he stopped?" Why did he say: "I have stopped"?

"Beauty is truth, truth beauty." She is going to classes in "health and beauty". He spoke of "truth", "beauty", "goodness". They said, "What do you mean by 'beauty' and 'truth'?"

Parentheses should be avoided wherever possible and commas used instead.

And, but, or These words are conjunctions. Their use at the beginning of a sentence, although legitimate, is best reserved for emphasis. Sentences usually read better without them at their head.

See also **accents**, **apostrophe**, **brackets**, **hyphens**, **italics**, **parentheses**, **quotation marks**.

puns are a splendid diversion for sub-editors but often irritate the reader. Do not use punning headlines except on light or humorous stories or features. If in doubt, avoid. If a pun is irresistible, make sure it is funny and in good taste.

Puritan an admirable 16th/17th-century religious group, not to be used as a contemporary adjective. Puritanical is just permitted.

purposes remove if needless, as in "land for development purposes", "water for washing purposes".

putsch is a military seizure of power, a violent coup. See also **coup**.

pygmy, pygmies are spelt thus.

Q

quality press use "serious" or better just "broadsheet", to contrast with "tabloid". See also **broadsheet**, **tabloid**.

quango quasi-autonomous nongovernment organisation. The word now tends to be used of any public sector body that is not a government department but is answerable to one, ie, not a nationalised industry.

quarter sessions are given thus.

Queen, the aim at retaining "the" in headlines. For Her Majesty the Queen, Her Majesty's inspectors, etc, use uc. Court Circular: follow copy style from the Palace press office. See also **palace**, **titles**.

Queen Elizabeth the Queen Mother no comma.

Queensberry, Marquess of and Queensberry Rules, but Queensbury, Yorkshire.

Queens' College Cambridge (plural) but Queen's College, Oxford; Queen's University, Belfast.

question a good specific word implying the need of an answer. Not to be overused as a synonym of problem, issue or some other evasion of concrete meaning. Say "question whether", not "question of whether" or "question as to whether".

quiet is a transitive verb, quieten is intransitive.

quota should mean allotted share and has no place in sentences such as: "Kew Gardens had its full quota of visitors". Use complement or share.

quotation marks (inverted commas) should be used with care. Use double quotation marks as standard, single only in headlines and for quotations within quotations. See also **headlines**, **italics**, **punctuation**.

1 Apart from their normal use in quotations, inverted commas should be used sparingly. Avoid using to imply some unspecified distancing from the words used. It is a bad habit, common in headlines, to use quotes to suggest that the thing mentioned was fake or misconceived: "'Bomb' in parcel", for an alarm clock that was mistaken for a bomb.

2 If a word forms part of the regular vocabulary of any

branch of human activity it can stand without quotes even if it is unfamiliar to most people. But a word such as "ornithopter", which has not yet been received into the language, if it must be used, should be put in quotes. So should slang and ad hoc formations such as "cowabunga".

3 If a remark or description is attributed to a speaker or document in reported speech, quotation marks are superfluous, eg, "He described the incident as outrageous" means exactly the same as "He described the incident as 'outrageous'".

4 Use with roman type for titles of paintings, drawings, sculptures, poems (unless the poem amounts to a book, eg, *Aeneid*), short stories, magazine articles and chapter headings.

quotes beware of the careless use of quoted remarks in the newspaper. Quotes should be corrected only to remove the solecisms and other errors that occur in speech but look silly in print. Always check that a quote is not defamatory. Quotes must be attributed to a person whose name is given in full at the first mention. Date and place should be included: "John Smith said yesterday afternoon at the scene of ...".

For unattributed quotes, see **Introduction**.

R

race nowadays such a loaded word that it is better replaced by people, nation, group. See also **blacks**.

racket for tennis, not racquet. The game is also rackets.

radio compounds are hyphenated when radio concerns wireless; single words when it concerns rays. Thus:

radio-telephony but radioactive, radioastronomy, radioisotope, radiotherapy, etc. Broadcasting frquencies are measured in megahertz (MHz) and kilohertz (kHz).

ranging from an uncomfortable phrase to be avoided except where there is some scale in which the things might be ranged, as in "ranging from ten to twelve years". A crowd "ranging from priests to golf professionals" is wrongly so described.

ranks (military and police): see **air force, military nomenclature, naval nomenclature, police ranks**.

re- see **hyphens**.

realistic is overworked, usually suggesting no more than the writer's approval of the idea expressed. Always try to make such adjectives more specific.

realpolitik roman type, not italic.

rebut means to argue to the contrary, producing evidence; to refute is to win such an argument. Rebut should not be used for deny, dispute or respond to.

receive injuries can be received, but broken limbs, heads, etc, ought not to be. For "he received (sustained) a broken leg" write "he broke his leg" or "his leg was broken".

recrudescence means worsening, and is what happens to wounds when they reopen and diseases that recur. In metaphor therefore it should be reserved for nasty contexts. The usage is wrong in "the recrudescence of public spirit among trade unionists", where resurgence or revival is meant.

reds (under beds), lc.

referendum plural referendums, as with conundrums, stadiums, forums and nearly all words ending in *-um*, but note millennia.

reflection spell thus except in some specific uses, when reflexion is correct.

refute see **rebut**.

Regent's Park is spelt thus.

register office is correct, but registry office is now so common a usage as to be acceptable.

Registrar (Oxford), Registrary (Cambridge).

relatively see **comparatively**.

remainder avoid as a synonym of "the rest".

Renaissance, the but lc renaissance as synonym of revival or rebirth, both of which are shorter and thus better.

rental rent is usually sufficient.

republican is lc unless in an official name, such as the US Republican party.

resolve usually as meaningless as the problem or issue or situation to which it is feebly attached. Use solve when you mean it.

respect of "in respect of" can usually be avoided, but never write "in respect to".

responsible people bear responsibility, things do not. Thunderstorms are not responsible for damage, they cause it. The IRA does not "claim responsibility" for a killing, it admits doing one.

result in perhaps the laziest of all verbs. "Resulted in" might replace all the verbs in the following passage: "The plague *caused* many deaths; it *created* alarm; it *evoked* public clamour; it *led to* an enquiry, it *brought about* reform". What a miserable passage it would become.

rethink why not "think again" or "second thoughts"?

Reuters the organisation is Reuters but convention attributes reports to Reuter, a Reuter report, etc.

Reverend see **church**.

rhetoric can be used as a synonym of both oratory and bombast. In the latter use, rhetoric has become cliché and should be avoided.

rhinoceroses are spelt thus.

Richter scale measures the amount of energy released by an earthquake. It runs from 0 to over 8. Write, "The earthquake measured 6 on the Richter scale".

right, the (political): the right wing, right-wing contenders, rightwingers, all lc.

riveting has one *t*, but however spelt, it is a cliché when used metaphorically.

roads it is tautologous to write M1 motorway or B262 road, but correct to refer to "the M25, London's orbital motorway" or "the A12 London to Colchester road". Always define a road geographically, except the best-known motorways, unless the context is clear.

rocks often used by Americans where the English word would be "stones". Avoid this use.

rococo a specific artistic style of the 18th century. It implies lightness, floridity and asymmetry in metaphor and is not a synonym of baroque.

Rolls-Royce (trade name) is uc and hyphenated.

Romania not Rumania.

Roman numerals no points except in side headings. Thus, Edward VIII, Article XVI, Part II, Psalm xxiii; but i., ii., iv., etc.

Romany technically more appropriate than gypsy. Refers to both the people and their language. See also **gypsy, traveller**.

rottweiler lc, if the brute really needs more publicity.

row used too often, not least in headlines, for a mere difference of opinion.

royal the royal family and royalty are lc. Always use lc for everyday adjectival uses of royal (the royal baby, the royal smile, a royal joke, etc). Royal is capitalised in titles, such as Royal Fine Art Commission, Royal Assent, Royal Household. For nomenclature see **titles**.

Royal Military Academy Sandhurst no comma.

royal standard only for the Sovereign. Other members of the royal family have a banner.

Royal Welch Fusiliers not Welsh.

RSPCA does not exist in Scotland, which has its own

organisation, the Scottish SPCA.

rue Royale etc takes lc for rue.

Russia, Russians Never use Russian when the person, place or event is plainly not Russian but Ukrainian, Georgian, etc, in which case specify the republic concerned. If a story refers to an ethnic Russian in a state such as Ukraine, this should be made clear. "Russian" can no longer be used an inclusive adjective, though Russian vodka is acceptable.

Avoid references to the "Soviet Union" or to "Soviet" except when the context is historical.

There is still no shorthand for the Commonwealth of Independent States. Use "the commonwealth" (lc) at second and subsequent mentions.

Stories should make clear the nationalities of future cosmonauts — if there are any.

When in doubt, consult *The Times* foreign desk.

S

sack avoid in the sense of dismiss, and beware of legal traps. Somebody who has resigned or been made redundant may sue if you write "sacked".

Sadler's Wells is spelt thus.

said an excellent word preferable to claimed, explained, declared, argued, but do not use for words that have been written, not spoken. Never start a sentence with said: "Said Mr Jones ...".

Saint is abbreviated to St, no full point.

St Albans no apostrophe.

St Andrews University no apostrophe.

St Giles' Cathedral (Edinburgh) apostrophe but no following *s*.

St Helens (Lancashire) no apostrophe.

St James's Palace apostrophe and following *s*.

St John Ambulance Brigade/Association no apostrophe.

St Katharine's Dock apostrophe.

St Martin-in-the-Fields no apostrophe, hyphenated.

St Neot (Cornwall) but St Neots (Cambridgeshire).

Saint-Saëns the composer is spelt thus.

St Stephen's Green (Dublin) not Stephen's Green.

saleroom is acceptable as one word.

salt water the noun is two words, the adjective saltwater is one.

Salvadorean not -*ian*.

sanction as a noun this means a constraint and is often misused in international relations. If the sanction is economic rather than military, you must call it so, preferably defining it further, as trade, credit, etc.

SAS see **military nomenclature**.

SBS see **naval nomenclature**.

scars do not heal despite constant journalistic therapy. Wounds heal, scars remain.

Scarborough (Yorkshire) is spelt thus.

schizophrenic is an adjective describing an illness. Do not use metaphorically or as term of abuse. See also **medical terms**.

Schleswig-Holstein is spelt thus.

schools see **education institutions, headmaster, public school**.

scientific measurements scientific units are internationally accepted and should be given correctly. Mistakes may alter meaning or make nonsense. Write out first time with abbreviation in parentheses, shorten subsequently. The abbreviation takes no point and no *s* in the plural. A scientific unit begins with a small letter even when named after a person, and does not usually carry diacritical marks, eg, Ampère for the man, ampere for the unit. The basic electrical units are abbreviated in capital letters.

When converting from one system of units to another, eg, from kilometres to miles, the final figure should not be carried to greater accuracy than is justified by the original figure. Thus, 15.2 km = 9.4 miles, but "about 10 km" = "about 6 miles". Note also that whereas 15 usually means "15 not 14 or 16", 15.0 means "15.0 not 14.9 or 15.1" and will be correct only in specific context.

See also **megawatts**.

1 Some basic international units and their abbreviations are: metre (m), gram (g), litre (l), ampere (A), volt (V), watt (W).

2 Prefixes are used to indicate multiples and sub-

multiples of scientific units. Thus: giga, a billion times; mega (M), a million times; kilo (k), a thousand times; milli (m), thousandth; micro, millionth; nano, billionth. Note that a prefix and unit form one word without a hyphen, eg, microsecond; there is danger of confusion between M and m; in abbreviation prefixes and units retain their respective large and small letters, eg, kilowatt-hour (kWh).

3 The following abbreviations of English units conflict with the international system and are incorrect: m for mile (except in mph, mpg, which are accepted); g for gram (should be gr); g for gallon (should be gal, except in mpg). Where *g* is used as a unit of acceleration, it should be italicised. Beware of using m for million in any scientific context, or for miles, when it might read as an abbreviation of metres.

Scilly, Isles of do not use "the Scilly Isles".

scotch this ancient trap still claims victims. Remember: "We have scotched the snake, not killed it". Various Shakespeareans have it as "scorched" or "put temporarily out of action". It does not mean stamp out, as in "The minister scotched rumours ...". Although this misuse may have become common usage (and may apply to rumours), it should be avoided.

Scotsman not Scotchman, Scottish not Scotch, the Scots not the Scotch, but Scotch whisky.

Scottish National Party but a Scottish nationalist (lc).

Scouts takes uc in Britain: no longer Boy Scouts but only Scouts; no Wolf Cubs, but Cub Scouts. Scoutmasters are now scoutleaders. In the USA there are still Boy Scouts, uc to avoid confusion. Ditto for Guides, Girl Guides.

Scripture is uc in Holy Scripture, but scriptural, lc.

SDI strategic defence initiative. Use in preference to "star wars".

seasons are always lc, spring, summer, etc.

seatbelt is one word.

second world war as time passes beware of "the last war". See also **postwar**.

Secretary of State is uc, but education secretary, lc. See also **capitalisation**.

seize not sieze.

semi- prefix meaning half, used before words of primarily Latin origin. Use hemi- for Greek roots. See also **demi-** and **hemi-**.

semi-colons see **punctuation**.

Senate (US) is uc. Senator Edward Kennedy but "the senator".

senior John Smith Sr, not Snr.

sequences a common error is to write such phrases as, "They arrived by bus, train and on bicycles". Whatever follows the *and* must conform to the opening series: either "They arrived by bus, train and bicycle" or "They arrived by bus, by train and on bicycles".

sergeant not serjeant. But Serjeant at Arms (no hyphens) and Serjeant's Inn.

serviceman, servicewoman one word.

set-up better avoided. Pick whichever is appropriate from arrangement, organisation, structure, system, etc.

sewage is the waste matter. Use sewerage for the disposal system.

sex see **obscenities**, **vice**.

sexism a delicate matter in the written word, given the masculine bias of some words and phrases. Without destroying idiom, we should be careful to avoid causing offence to women. See **bisexual pronouns**, **boy friend**, **feminine designations**, **girl**, **lady**, **Ms**.

shaikh not sheikh, and lc except as a title with a name.

Shakespearean, not -*ian*.

shall, should have always been vigorously defended by *The Times* against *will* and *would*. Good practice is that *shall* and *should* go with the first persons singular and plural, *will* and *would* with the others: I shall, he will, we shall, they will. The use of *shall* with second and third persons singular and plural has a slightly more emphatic meaning, and this distinction is therefore useful. By extension, "I will" is seen as less emphatic than "I shall". MacArthur's "I shall return" is a firm intention; "I will return" would be merely a prediction. Common usage also gives *should* a measure of moral force, while *would* is acquiring a mild conditionality. Use these words with discrimination.

shambles is singular. It means a slaughterhouse and, by extension, a scene of carnage. It should not be used lightly in metaphor. "When the lights went out the church social was reduced to a shambles" is implausible though not inconceivable.

she see **bisexual pronouns**.

Shepherds Bush no apostrophe.

Shetland and the Shetland Islands, not the Shetlands.

Shia not Shi'ite, and be careful to add Muslim(s). The two main groups are Shia Muslims and Sunni Muslims.

shock avoid whenever possible, even in headlines, to mean an unpleasant surprise. Never use as a modifier: "shock revelations", etc.

Siam now Thailand. Use Siamese for twins and cats, otherwise Thai.

siege (not seige): do not misuse for an occupation or sit-in unless those involved are besieged.

singular always preferable to plural, use for institutions, corporate bodies, government departments. See also **collective nouns, plurals**.

sink, sank the past participle is sunk, the adjective sunken.

Sinn Fein, Sinn Feiners are given thus.

siphon is spelt thus.

Site of Special Scientific Interest (SSSI) capitalise such mouthfuls only where confusion might otherwise result. The abbreviation on subsequent mention is capitalised.

situation avoid. Even a quote using this vacuous word is probably waffle and not worth quoting. The word situation cannot be rescued by being propped up by an adjective, as in "classroom situation", let alone the *banned* "crisis situation". As for ongoing situation, no-win situation and chicken-and-egg situation ...!

sizable not sizeable.

ski, skied, skier, skiing are spelt thus.

skulduggery is spelt thus.

Slovak see **Czechoslovakia**.

smelt not smelled.

snarl-up an awful substitute for traffic jam, confusion, etc.

so never use as alternative to the banned *very* in headlines "So cool vicar to wed nurse" is strictly for the tabloid press.

soccer the word football is preferable unless there is a risk of confusion with rugby. See also **sporting terms**.

socialist capitalise only if attachment to a Socialist party is directly implied, eg, a Socialist deputy. But lc for socialist ideals, socialist state, socialist MP (in Britain), if distinguished from the preferable Labour MP.

Socialist party (British): use Labour party, especially as there is a small Socialist Party of Great Britain (SPGB), itself prone to frequent subdivision and resulting confusion.

so far as so-and-so is concerned this is nearly always unnecessary and is best avoided. Often an ordinary preposition is enough. Not "The subject is unknown so far as astronomy is concerned", but "... is unknown to astronomy".

Solicitor General takes uc, no hyphen.

SOS no points and close up.

Sotheby's has an apostrophe.

south, the lc except where the phrase has specific meaning, eg, the South in stories about America or Ireland. See also **compass points**.

South Africa has three capital cities: Pretoria (administrative), Cape Town (legislative), Bloemfontein (judicial). Pretoria is usually referred to as the seat of government.

South Asia encompasses the following states: Afghanistan, Bangladesh, Bhutan, India, Maldives, Nepal, Pakistan, Sri Lanka.

southeast, southwest, southeasterly etc, one word. See also **compass points**.

Southeast Asia encompasses the ASEAN states, ie, Brunei, Indonesia, Malaysia, Philippines, Singapore, Thailand, and also Burma, Cambodia, Laos and Vietnam.

southern Africa usually refers to Africa south of the Congo/Zambezi rivers.

Southwest Africa is now Namibia.

Sovereign, the takes uc. See also **Queen, the**.

Soviet Union see **Russia**.

space may be described as interplanetary, interstellar or extragalactic (outside this galaxy). None is empty. Do not say "outer space". In this context, Earth, Sun and Moon always take uc to avoid confusion.

Spanish surnames usually double-barrelled and both are normally used on second reference; if only one, it is the first barrel. But there are exceptions, including Picasso, Lorca and the prime minister, Felipe Gonzalez. In Portugal the rules are more complex, so use the full name, even if this means three every time. See also **appellations**.

spastic not spasdic, and never use figuratively. See also **medical terms**.

Speaker, the (in the House of Commons) takes uc.

species is both the singular and plural form for the groups of plants, animals, etc, defined as capable of breeding fertile offspring. The word specie is used only of minted metal (coins or medals) as opposed to bullion.

spelt not spelled.

spilt not spilled.

Spiritualism, Spiritualist take uc.

split infinitives never, except in famous quotes such as "to boldly go where no man ..." or in such limited emphatic constructions as "I want to live–to *really* live!"

spoilt not spoiled (but despoiled).

spokesman an ugly word, as is spokeswoman (which may be used), so avoid whenever possible. Use "an official said".

sporting terms sports writing is notoriously vulnerable to cliché. Great sports writing is writing that invents its own imagery. Refer to women's (not ladies') competitions, championships, events. Note the following terms, spellings, etc.

Baseball inning (not innings).

Boxing featherweight, heavyweight, etc, (one word); light-heavyweight, knockout(s).

Cricket wicketkeeper, mid-off, mid-wicket, follow on (verb and noun), hit-wicket, mis-hit, third man, extra cover, off-break, leg-before, a four (not 4). An off spinner is a bowler who bowls off-breaks. Delivery in cricket is a bowling action, not a ball: "Hollies has a puzzling delivery", not "Hollies bowled Jenkins with his first delivery".

The governing body for cricket in England is the Cricket Council. The Test and County Cricket Board (TCCB) controls the professional and commercial side of the game. The MCC is concerned with the rules of cricket and with domestic matters at Lord's.

Football by itself means the Association game. Use soccer only when needed to differentiate from rugby or other forms of football. Never use the word rugger. In Association football: goalkeeper, kick-off (noun), Arsenal (not *the*), midfield, offside. In Rugby Union (or Rugby League) football: full back, stand-off half, touchdown, knock-on, scrummage, threequarter, open-side flanker, lineout(s), on-side, 22-metre line, the 22.

Golf The holes should appear in text and results as 1st, 2nd, 10th, 18th, but write the "third extra hole" after that. In a match-play use, "Jones beat Brown 2 and 1" (not two and one). Note the following style: "Nicklaus holed a six-foot [12-foot] putt. Faldo holed from eight [15] feet." See also **numbers**.

Bogey, birdie, eagle (no quotes). Dormy, only if the match can be halved: a player cannot be dormy if the match can be taken to, say, the 19th hole to reach a decision.

Swimming freestyle, backstroke, breaststroke are all one word.

Yachting America's Cup.

Sri Lanka official name for Ceylon; adjective, Sri Lankan.

stalemate is better avoided in the sense of deadlock. See also **chess**.

stanch is a verb, the adjective is staunch.

star wars avoid, use strategic defence initiative (SDI on second reference).

state always lc except when part of an official name: Council of State. Thus, state medicine, state occasion, the state takes half, welfare state, etc.

Stationery Office not HMSO, except after documents.

statistic never use as just a fancy word for figure or number, whether singular or plural.

status quo roman, but the less familiar *status quo ante* in italics.

statute book is given thus.

Stock Exchange takes uc, but stock market.

storey of a building, and *-eys*, *-eyed*.

straight do not use for heterosexual. See also **gay**.

straitjacket is one word, but straight-faced, strait-laced, in dire straits.

stratum is singular, the plural is strata.

strong try to avoid compound numerals with -*strong* to make unwieldy adjectives, as in "The 100-strong rebel group of MPs". Write: "A group of 100 rebel MPs".

sub- as a general rule, avoid a hyphen with this and other prefixes unless the resulting compound might look or sound odd. Hence subcommittee, subdivision, sublet, subnormal, subsection, substandard, but sub-editor, sub-postmaster, sub-post office. See also **hyphens**.

subject see **citizen**.

submarine always a boat, never a ship. See also **naval nomenclature**.

subpoena subpoenas, subpoenaing, subpoenaed.

subsequently the words afterwards or later are preferable. Avoid "subsequent to" for "after".

substantial like considerable and major, suggests the writer is too genteel or timid to write the word big or large.

such as do not confuse with *like*.

Sudan not *the* Sudan.

summon the verb is to summon, the noun a summons (plural summonses). A person is summoned to appear before a tribunal, etc. However, summons is a verb and those in receipt of a specific summons can be said to have been summonsed.

sun, the usually lc, but uc when in an astronomical context. See also **space**.

super is overworked in the formation of new compounds or as an adjective to indicate something or someone above the average. Avoid in this sense, and also the newly fashionable mega- and even giga-.

superlatives where comparatives are usually sloppy, superlatives are usually dangerous. Beware of calling any person, event or thing the first, biggest, best or most significant without evidence or checking your facts. See also **universal and absolute claims**.

supersonic means above the speed of sound and is a cliché in metaphor.

sustain a broken leg is pompous: just break a leg.

swap not swop. Do not use unless a mutual exchange is involved and never for organ transplants.

switch (intransitive), avoid in the sense of change or shift.

synod is lc except when part of an official title. See also **capitalisation, church**.

T

-t where there is a choice of past tense between a final *-t* or *-ed*, use *-t* as in burnt, spelt, etc.

tabloid now common usage for a half-broadsheet newspaper. "Tabloid journalism" is a cliché. See also **broadsheet, quality press**.

takeover (noun), but to take over (verb).

take place a dull substitute for too many verbs that give life to a description of a happening. If simplicity is required use that splendid and oft-neglected verb, to be.

taoiseach the Irish prime minister.

tattoos is spelt thus.

taxes lc, no hyphens; income tax, value added tax (VAT), etc. On subsequent mentions, do not write VAT tax, just VAT.

Tchaikovsky is spelt thus.

teams normally plural (England were beaten, Arsenal are struggling). See also **collective nouns**.

Teesside no hyphen.

Tehran not Teheran.

telephone numbers with three groups of figures, hyphenate the first two (061-834 1234). With a place-name, use parentheses for the code: Uptown (0232) 1234.

television abbreviate to TV only in headlines where necessary. Refer to commercial television as independent television (lc) or ITV in headlines, but "the commercial television companies" is correct. Independent Television News (ITN) is uc.

temperature use style 30°C, 80°F. Both celsius and fahrenheit should still be given in news stories.

terrorism beware this overused word. It means the generation of widespread fear for political ends such as bombing civilian areas and should be avoided as a synonym of murder, killing, bombing or other violence. Do not use for any dissident group, which may have used violence, that the writer dislikes. Few groups are "terrorist organisations". They are paramilitary, or political, or gangster organisations that may commit acts of civil terror to further their aims. Do not grace them with this possibly glamorous name.

Test match the word Test takes uc. See also **sporting terms**.

Thailand is the country, the people are Thai. See also **Siam**.

Thamesmead but Thames-side.

thank-offering is hyphenated.

that almost always better than *which* in a defining clause: "The train that I take stops at Slough". As a general rule use *which* for descriptive clauses and place it between commas: "The night train, which used to carry mail and newspapers, stops at Crewe". The distinction is worth observing, as "The night train that used to carry mail and newspapers stops at Crewe" implies that there is more than one night train. Note that *that* is not incorrect for persons: "He that hath ears to hear", and can avert the need for an inelegant *whom*, as in "The witness that the police needed".

the see **definite article**.

their see **bisexual pronouns**.

the then avoid expressions such as "the then Mr Callaghan", "the then Lord Chancellor". Use "the Chancellor at the time", or "Lord Callaghan (then Mr Callaghan)".

The Times is italicised. Keep references to the paper to a minimum. Avoid "so-and-so told *The Times*", prefer "said". Avoid *we* and *us* in reference to the paper, except rarely in eccentric cases such as third leaders. We do not "exclusively reveal" or even "reveal". Everything in the paper should be a revelation. The company that publishes *The Times* is Times Newspapers Ltd. See also **News International**.

thin on the ground why not scarce?

Throne capitalise when meaning the institution, lc when the chair.

thunderbolts are mythological and do not exist. Lightning bolts and thunder-claps do exist and can be used metaphorically.

Tirol not Tyrol and not *the* Tirol.

titles almost every surname should be granted the courtesy of a title. When mentioning titled people in *The Times*, avoid such clichés as giving their seal, family motto, ancestors or relatives, unless relevant to the story. Follow carefully the guidelines given below. All titles should be checked in Debrett's *Peerage*, *Who's Who* or similar reference books. Note that baronets, knights and dames take their appropriate title as soon as the honour is announced. Peers have to submit their choice of title for approval. This is not known until a public announcement is made, usually in *The London Gazette*. Until then they remain Mr, etc (but mention peerage award in parentheses). Honorifics such as Right Hon for privy counsellors, judges, etc are used only in the Court Circular.

1 The royal family
The Sovereign is styled the Queen (not Her Royal Highness or Her Majesty except in official statements).

The Duke of Edinburgh and the Prince of Wales may
be referred to as Prince Philip and Prince Charles
respectively after the first mention, or as the duke and
the prince. Use Princess of Wales, not Princess Diana,
and the princess after first mention. Use the Duke of
York for Prince Andrew, the duke thereafter. His wife is
the Duchess of York, the duchess thereafter. Queen
Elizabeth the Queen Mother (no comma) at first
mention, the Queen Mother thereafter. Princess Anne is
known as the Princess Royal, the princess thereafter.
Princess Alexandra, omit the Hon Mrs Angus Ogilvy
except in official statements on the Court page.

2 Peers

Dukes are referred to as "the Duke of ...", and "the
duke" after the first mention.

Marquesses, earls, viscounts and barons All ranks
of the peerage below that of duke are normally given
their full title on first mention, and styled "Lord ..."
thereafter. Barons are always referred to as "Lord ..."
never baron. Life peers include women, who are called
Baroness Smith, not Lady Smith. Avoid calling them
life peeresses. Remember "peer" strictly refers only to
those entitled to sit in the House of Lords. No peer takes
a Christian name with his title. The description of Lord
Willis as "Lord Ted Willis" is impermissible. If a peer
wishes to be known professionally by his previous name,
respect that wish.

Titles and place-names In modern creations the
title is followed, after a comma, by a territorial
designation that may itself consist of a surname and a
place-name. In such cases there is no comma until the
title itself is complete and the territorial designation
begins, eg, Viscount Montgomery of Alamein, of
Hindhead in the county of Surrey; Lord Bridge of
Harwich, of Harwich in the county of Essex.

When the title includes a place-name do not omit it
in the first mention. This is particularly important in
such cases as Lord Harris of Greenwich and Lord

Harris of High Cross, who are different peers.

Some peers' titles have a different spelling from the modern place-name, eg, the Earl of Guilford (after whom Guilford Street is named), but Guildford; the Marquess of Donegall, but co. Donegal, etc.

Wives and children of peers The eldest son of a duke can be an earl or a marquess (check individual titles in Debrett). The eldest son of a marquess is an earl. The eldest son of an earl is Lord Smith (normally the family name). All sons of viscounts are Honourables. The younger sons of dukes and marquesses are Lord (John Smith). The younger sons of earls and marquesses are Honourables.

The daughters of dukes, marquesses and earls are Lady (Jane Smith). The daughters of marquesses are Honourables.

Wives of younger sons of dukes and marquesses are known as Lady (Jane Smith); if she marries she changes only her surname unless her husband is a peer. Lord John Smith and his wife may be referred to as Lord John and Lady John respectively after first mention; together they are styled Lord and Lady John Smith. Lady Jane may be thus referred to after her full name has been given, whether she is single or married. She and her husband, if a commoner, are referred to as Mr James and Lady Jane Jones, or as Sir James and Lady Jane Jones if he is a knight or baronet.

Widows and former wives of peers may place their Christian names, without a comma, in front of their former husband's title, eg, Jane Duchess of Barchester, or they may style themselves Lady Jane Smith. A widow may prefer to call herself a dowager, eg, the Dowager Duchess of Barchester.

3 Other titles
Baronets and knights are known as Sir John Smith, Sir John after first mention. No wife or widow of a baronet or knight takes her Christian name in her title unless she is a daughter of a duke, marquess or earl. If a

knight has had more than one wife, by social usage
former wives put their Christian names in brackets:
Lady (Alice) Brown to distinguish her from the present
wife, who is Lady Brown. If there are two knights or
baronets with the same surname, their wives, when
mentioned apart from their husbands, put his Christian
name in brackets: Lady (Henry) Brown and Lady (John)
Brown.

Dames of an order of chivalry take the same style as
knights, ie, Dame Felicity Brown, referred to as Dame
Felicity after first mention. A dame who is married may
prefer to use her own style, eg, Dame Jennifer Jenkins,
wife of Lord Jenkins. Their personal preferences should
be respected.

tomatoes are spelt thus.

tornado plural, tornados: both storm and aircraft.

totalisator, tote takes lc, no quotes, but the Tote (uc)
refers to the organisation.

towards not toward.

trade names many names of products in common use
are proprietary and require a capital letter. Beware of
misuses, which may be actionable, eg, Biro,
Cinemascope, Dictaphone, Hoover (vacuum cleaner),
Hovercraft, Jeep, Kodak, Land-Rover, Perspex,
Polaroid, Tannoy (loudspeaker), Technicolor, Thermos,
Walkman, Xerox, Yale lock (never say Yale-type lock for
other makes: they are called cylinder-rim locks). Since
their mention is a free advertisement it is better to avoid
them if possible. Be especially careful of drugs; always
try to use a non-proprietary name, such as aspirin,
sleeping pill, etc.

trade union not trades union, plural trade unions, but

Trades Union Congress. Note General Council of the TUC (uc), but general council (lc) by itself.

tranquilliser is spelt thus.

transatlantic, transcontinental are spelt thus.

transistor is a component in electronic apparatus, such as radio sets; its use on its own to mean portable radio should be avoided.

transpire means to come to light or leak out. Do not use as a genteel alternative to happen or occur or be.

trans-ship use hyphen.

Transvaal but Transvaler.

traveller see **gypsy, Romany**.

trillion is the American for a thousand billion. If used in stories about the American or Japanese budgets, this must be explained. Britain is not yet so extravagant as to need it, so avoid in home stories.

tripos is lc, but the History Tripos, etc.

Trooping the Colour not *of* the Colour.

Trustee Savings Bank see **TSB**.

tsar (not czar), tsarevich, tsaritsa (not czarina). As with other titles, lc on their own, capitalised with name.

TSB use TSB Bank plc and TSB thereafter.

T-shirt not teeshirt.

Tube use the London Tube (uc) or the London Underground. Tube once referred only to the deep tunnelled lines, but this is now a pedantic distinction.

tuberculosis the adjective is tuberculous, not tubercular.

tunku (Malayan prince): lc on its own, capitalised before name.

turn down prefer reject or refuse, except of beds.

TV use television, except in headlines.

U

U no full point after Burmese prefix, eg, U Nu.

Ukraine not *the* Ukraine.

Ulster see **Northern Ireland**.

Ulster Defence Regiment (UDR), a former component of the British army, now merged with a mainland regiment. The UDA, UVF, etc, are illegal, paramilitary organisations. They should be described as such. See also **Irish Republican Army, Loyalist, Northern Ireland, terrorism**.

ultimate avoid overuse. "He finally reached the ultimate limits of his endurance" presumably means he died. Ultimate limit means limit.

ultimatums not -*a*.

unchristian is lc thus. See also **Christian**.

uncoordinated one word, no hyphen (but co-ordinate).

undeceived is a Janus word. To undeceive can mean to inform someone of a mistake or to leave them in a false state of belief. "She shook her head, undeceived," (*Blind Witness*). Agatha Christie meant she was not deceived, but she could have meant that she had just been informed about something. Such nuances can matter in detective stories, and elsewhere.

Underground see **Tube**.

understudy do not call an established actor who replaces another an understudy. He or she is a replacement.

underwater as adjective is one word.

under way two words, and remember that only boats "get under way". Prefer start or begin, but "the meeting was well under way when ..." is acceptable.

Union Jack except in naval and some ceremonial contexts when Union Flag is correct.

unique means one of a kind. It is therefore nonsense to describe something as rather unique, more unique. However, the phrase "almost unique", while strictly a contradiction in terms, does convey a specific meaning and is acceptable as common usage.

United Nations or the UN. Unesco, Unifil, etc, where the word is voiced. See also **capitalisation**.

United Reformed Church not "Reform". See also **church**.

United States (of America) is followed by a singular

verb. Abbreviated to US only in headlines and uses such as US Navy. See **American** for US as an adjective.

universal and absolute claims subjects about which it is true to say "everybody agrees that ..." or "no one will dispute that ..." are few indeed. Be careful with these expressions. Care must also be taken in asserting that such-and-such is the first or last of its kind, or that so-and-so was the first person to ..., or the last surviving member of ... Such assertions lead to countless mistakes and tedious corrections. See also **of all time**, **superlatives**.

university lc except in official names, eg, the University of Kent.

University College London no comma.

up beware superfluous use in phrasal verbs, as in meet up, rest up, end up. Drop it.

upon distinguish the fine differences with up on, up and on. The cat jumped *on* the floor, *upon* the mouse, *up on* the table, *up* the tree. See also **into**.

US see **United States** and **American**.

utilise why not *use*?

V

vacuum a verb in common usage, but avoid Hoover; see also **trade names**.

vagaries means aimless wanderings, not vicissitudes or changes (as in weather).

Valletta (Malta) is spelt thus.

Van in Dutch names is capitalised when the surname alone is given, as in Van Gogh, but lc when used in full, Vincent van Gogh. See also **von**.

Van Dyck, Sir Anthony but vandyke brown, vandyke beard, etc.

various is not a pronoun. "Various of the countries concerned protested ..." is wrong. Write "Many of the ...".

VAT value-added tax (all lc), spell out on first mention, VAT thereafter. See also **taxes**.

veld not veldt.

verbal means pertaining to words (contrasted with, say, physical or choral). It does not mean spoken. Sadly, sportsmen have made common usage of "verbal abuse" and "verbal warning". "Oral abuse" would sound odd, however, and the best rule is to confine verbal to contexts in which a contrast is drawn with non-verbal communication.

verbs are the journalist's best friend. See also **Introduction**.

very occasions when very helps a following word are rare. Its constant use inflates language without strengthening its meaning. In giving up very, do not turn nervously to highly or most. Have confidence in your choice of the main words in a sentence to do the job you expect of them. Always delete very and then see if it is really needed. That said, do not strip your writing of all idiom: "She seems *very* English to me". "Nice? Not *very*!"

viable should be restricted to the sense of capable of independent existence. It is not a substitute for feasible or practicable.

vice we should hold out against the practice, which comes from the exigencies of headline writing of limiting the word vice to sex. It is the opposite to virtue and correspondingly wide in meaning.

video normally followed by -tape, -recorder or -recording. However, common usage now regards video as a noun, meaning both a movie tape cassette and the machine in which it is played.

Vietnam not Viet nam.

Virgil not Vergil.

virtu object of, not virtue here: anything that might appeal to a collector or connoisseur.

viscountcy describes the rank; see also **titles**.

viz avoid; use namely, that is to say or (sparingly) ie.

vogue words wander in and out of journalism and can become instant clichés. They are as likely to deaden a story as to enliven it. The only safe rule is to beware of them. Current examples: backlash, bombshell, bonanza, brainchild, charisma, "Cinderella of", consensus, crunch, escalate, facelift, lifestyle, mega-, persona, prestigious, quantum leap, rationale, trauma(tic), viable.

von (German) is lc: omit when surname stands by itself. See also **Van**.

W

warfarin not a trade name, so lc.

warn is strictly a transitive verb needing an object. Ideally the prime minister thus cannot "warn about inflation", but should "give a warning" or "warn the nation about inflation". That said, the object of the warning is, in common usage, often assumed. "The monarch should warn as well as advise" is acceptable.

wars lc as in the first world war, Vietnam war, Hundred Years war, Cold war. But Great War (the first world war).

wartime one word.

waste, wastage before writing wastage ask yourself whether waste is not better. Wastage means the process of loss, or its amount or rate.

watercolour(s), watercolourist but Royal Society of Painters in Water Colours.

week this ends on Saturday night but, in Saturday's paper, last week clearly does refer back to the preceding six days. The best guide is to treat Saturday and Sunday as today and tomorrow, and treat the past and the next week as the preceding and succeeding seven days. Last week is acceptable, but see **last, past**.

weekend one word.

weights and measures it is no longer necessary to convert metric measures into their "imperial" equivalent, unless to help the sense of a story. See also **scientific measurements**, **temperature**.

Welch, Welsh Royal Welch Fusiliers, but Welsh Guards.

Welsh Office is uc, but Welsh secretary is u/lc.

Welsh words *-dd*, *-ff*, *-ll*, *-ng*, *-ch* should not be separated at the end of a line. Always check Welsh spellings.

West, the is uc, as are Western leaders, but be careful of whom you are including as the East changes fast. See also **compass points**, **East**.

Western Isles not the Hebrides.

West Germany no longer exists. Use only in a historical context. See also **Germany**.

whereabouts treat as singular, eg, "His whereabouts is not known". But prefer, "Nobody knows where he is".

which see **that**.

while not whilst.

whiskey (Irish and American), but whisky (other types).

white paper (government) is lc.

who, whom remember that the case of the relative pronoun is determined solely by its function in the relative clause. "Give it to whomever wants it" is a common mistake for "... to whoever wants it". "Whom do you think did it?" should also be "Who ...".

wide no hyphen in compounds such as countrywide, nationwide, worldwide.

wideawake always one word, though fast asleep is two.

widow of John Jones not of the late John Jones.

wildfowl, wildlife one word.

Winchester College its pupils are Wykehamists.

wind with strong winds, give a description as well as force number, in numerals, "storm force 10" on the Beaufort scale.

Wolf Cubs now called Cub Scouts. See also **Scouts**.

woman doctors, teachers not women ... See also **feminine designations, lady**.

wordy phrases such as *on the part of* for *by*; *a great deal* for *much*; *a large number* for *many*; *numerous occasions* for *many times*; and meaningless, vague ones such as *a number of, within minutes, this day and age* should be rooted out from all stories. They are the weeds and tares of good style.

world avoid, if possible, the fashion world, football world, theatre world, etc.

World War I/II use first world war/second world war.

worth while is often used when worth by itself is called for: "The programme was worth recording", not "The programme was worth while recording". Worthwhile (one word) is used only in front of a noun, eg, "a worthwhile journey".